THIS DARNED ELUSIVE
HAPPINESS

THÉUN MARES

*With all my love
to all of you hunters out there.
Théun*

THIS DARNED ELUSIVE
HAPPINESS

THÉUN MARES

Lionheart
PUBLISHING

OTHER BOOKS BY THÉUN MARES

Return of the Warriors
Cry of the Eagle
The Mists of Dragon Lore

What people have been saying about Theun's work...

"Required reading for anyone serious about really living life".

"I love his sense of humour and adaptability to everyday life situations".

"These books changed my life".

"I bought your book about 4 weeks ago now...what resulted was a 'magical journey', which continues today".

ABOUT THE AUTHOR

Born in Zimbabwe, Théun's father was a miner and his mother a teacher. He spent most of his early life in the bush, among the animals and the natives of the area, with their rich and abundant folklore.

It was in these early years that his quest for knowledge began – a quest which was to lead him to reject much of conventional wisdom and to embrace instead alternative ways of understanding the world.

Because he grew up with African children and had never thought of them as anything but his equals, it came as a shock to Théun when he first encountered racism. "It was really that that got me questioning so many things in life, not only racial prejudice, but also so much else concerning life and how we have all been socially conditioned in our views on life."

During his first year at university, Théun came to the realisation that if he was ever going to find answers to these questions, he was going to have to look for them himself. "It dawned on me that the only way in which I could do that was to start to re-assess and re-evaluate everything I had learnt in my life."

Following university Théun's career took him into the performing arts and then into education. In these fields Théun gained a wealth of experience in the behaviour and interactions between different types of people, different classes, cultures and backgrounds, as well as different age groups.

He believes that such diversity, which is the hallmark of South Africa, is also its greatest strength, for it is only by fully exploring and understanding differences that true unity of purpose can come into being.

He now divides his time between teaching individuals, writing books and training courses, and lives in Cape Town with Marianne, who is playing a vital role in ensuring the balance between the male and the true female.

This book is dedicated to my greater family, those wonderful creatures called human beings, who in spite of being quite the funniest of all species on this earth, sadly seem to have lost touch with their innate sense of what constitutes genuine fun and lasting joy.

© Théun Mares 1999

All rights reserved. No part of this book may be reproduced by any means or in any form whatsoever without written permission from the publisher, except for brief quotations embodied in literary articles or reviews.

ISBN 1-919792-03-1

Cover concept by: Martin Grafetsberger & Debra Berry
Cover illustration by: Alice Barry
DTP & illustrations by: Alice Barry

Printed and bound by:
Cape & Transvaal Book Printers, Parow, Cape

PUBLISHED BY:

Lionheart
PUBLISHING

Private Bag X5,
Constantia
7848
Cape Town
South Africa
Phone: +27 21 794-4923
FAX: +27 21 794-1487
e-mail: cajmi@iafrica.com
web: www.elusivehappiness.com

CONTENTS

Preface	1
Introduction	4
Chapter 1	6

Relating to life
What is life?

Chapter 2	12

The journey of adjustment & The 4 Terms of Captain Life

Chapter 3	16

Term 1: Becoming aware of another's state of being
- Using fear
- Developing respect
- The differences between male & female
- Using your own knowledge
- Feelings & emotions are not the same
- What is true love?
- Understanding mirrors
- The world is filled with mothers & little boys

Chapter 4
57

Term 2: Changing your self-image
- Achieving harmony through conflict
- Whilst man & woman relate to gender, the terms male & female relate to specific states of awareness
- The role of the hunter
- The rules of intelligent co-operation
- Using conflict to uncover new knowledge

Chapter 5
99

Term 3: Your shortcomings are your ticket to freedom
- Working consciously with mirrors
- The art of listening
- The secret of unconditional love
- Compromise versus sacrifice

Chapter 6
130

Term 4: Give yourself time

Chapter 7
132

The rules for playing the game of relationships

Chapter 8
138

The password for life and for happiness

PREFACE

What would you say to someone who told you that the key to happiness was sitting right under your nose, and that it had always been there? When the author of this book, Théun Mares, first told me that, I felt somewhat frustrated and disappointed. Nevertheless, I decided to humour him and not say anything at all in the hope that he would in time reveal the real secrets. Meanwhile, I carried on my search for happiness, with my eyes firmly fixed on the horizon. However, like the horizon, happiness kept moving back with each step forward that I took.

Luckily for me, I happen also to be a student of Théun's, as well as his publisher, and since I could see that he did not appear to struggle at all with being happy in his life, I decided to start to take notice of what he had been telling me. Nevertheless, it took a while before I was able to see the truth in what he had said. It seems that this is a common problem, because we have an acquired tendency to discount the obvious and the commonplace, and instead to reach for complicated answers. In our rush for technological and academic achievement, we have become too "clever" for our own good and we tend to rationalise more and more about life, with the result that true happiness slips through our fingers.

Through working and studying with Théun I have developed the guiding principle now that one does not need to have any academic qualifications at all in order to understand how to live and how to get the most out of life. The keys to life and to happiness have to be within the reach and the abilities of even the simplest person, otherwise there would be no point to life. Therefore, rather than acquiring new tricks, the secret is to discard an enormous amount of what we have been taught about life.

However, even though the keys to happiness may be simple, this does not mean that they are easy. In fact, putting them into practice is often fiendishly difficult, as there always seems to be a gap between what we know we should do and what we have made a lifetime's habits of doing.

What I have discovered in my association with Théun is that although there are no quick fixes on the path to happiness, once we make a decision to start on our journey, with a few tools in our pocket, life is never the same. Sometimes we fly, sometimes we crash, but we travel under our own power, and that's what gives life a new dimension of exhilaration, of excitement. To develop the confidence and the belief in oneself to say "Yes! I did it all my own way", is, for me, what makes every day different and worthwhile. The effect of this is that whether it is sunny or cloudy, you learn to make your own weather.

Over time, I have found that the principles explained in this book have lead me to a different understanding of the meaning of happiness. I have learned that happiness, far from being on the horizon, is all around us — it just needs to be grasped consciously. It really is as simple, but also as difficult, as making a choice to live, for once one chooses life, one also chooses happiness.

The reason why so many people love watching sport is not so much for the end result, for the victory, but because they want to share, vicariously, in each step of the battle — a battle in which seconds seem to be measured in minutes, as excitement and intensity are locked into focus whilst each side, or player, gives it their all.

Similarly, when we choose for happiness and for life, it is the intensity and passion that we generate during each step of our own battles that is remembered. Victories come and go, but what we can get out of each battle is never lost.

So, for me, choosing life has turned out to be a very practical affair, which involves learning to be nimble and alert and passionate enough about life to be able to catch hold of that elusive happiness which is always, in spite of appearances, present in each of our encounters, every day of our lives.

I hope that your own voyage of discovery is as exciting and rewarding as it has so far been for me.

Charles Mitchley
Cape Town

INTRODUCTION

There are several different ways in which I could have presented the material here, but because this book is meant to put people back in touch with what it means to have genuine fun and to experience lasting joy, I made the decision to take a fun approach. As a result, technicalities are either ignored or else brushed over, for as we all know, fun is dependent upon feeling, rather than juggling intellectual concepts. However, for those readers who would like a deeper insight into the material contained in this book, my other books will prove to be a help.

I have placed the accent throughout this book, not on those huge boulders which are clear for everyone to see, but on those tiny irritating little pebbles which cause most of us to stumble and fall, simply because, being so apparently insignificant, we did not even see them to start with. Think for a moment. How many times a day do you have a car accident? But how many times a day do you have an "accident" with another person by inadvertently putting your foot in it and then, by trying to extricate yourself, you only seem to dig yourself in deeper? Does that sound familiar? If so, this book is for you.

This book is all about shifting the focus, about saying good-bye to Misery and saying hello to Happiness. So let us bury Cousin Misery right here and now, and let us plant upon her grave all the seeds of happiness you have always longed for.

Yet one word of caution is still called for. Before you can plant any seeds, you must be quite sure that you do indeed want to bury old Cousin Misery, for if you do not bury her, she will continue to drain you, and you will be forced to keep her sustained with every scrap of temporary happiness you may be able to find. You see, this is the nature of life: *we choose to be happy, or we choose to be miserable, but in both instances the amount of effort required is the same.* So, either way, irrespective of what your choice is, enjoy this book, for such is its purpose!

ONE

RELATING TO LIFE

Today is the first day of the rest of your life.

I don't know who said that, but somehow it makes a great deal of sense. To me it means that irrespective of how badly we may have screwed up yesterday, or last week, or last year, today is the day on which we are going to put the past behind us, not in the sense of brushing it under the carpet, but in the sense of not allowing it to keep making us miserable. We always have the choice either of being thoroughly ashamed and guilty about our past actions, or of looking upon our past actions objectively and honestly enough to be able to own them.

Owning our actions does not mean that we are necessarily proud of them, but it does mean that we are honest and honourable enough to admit that we screwed up, but that we are willing to take full responsibility for our actions. By taking responsibility for our actions, we not only own them, but we also claim them in terms of the knowledge we have gained through our experience.

Knowledge gained through experience cannot possibly be

bad, unless, of course, we use that knowledge to perpetuate our wrong actions, either towards others or towards ourselves. However, if I have burned my fingers in one way or another, and own that experience, then I can use the knowledge I have gained not to burn myself again, and I can also use that knowledge to warn others of the dangers of walking into that trap. Alternatively, I can use that knowledge to be a support to those around me who have likewise burned their fingers, and to give them guidance based upon my own experience.

It is true that not all knowledge is beautiful, and not all experience fills us with a sense of pride and accomplishment, but the truth is that there are no angels on this earth. Some of us may appear to be very sanctified, but that is simply because we have learned to do one of two things; either we hide our skeletons better than anyone else, or, by owning our actions and our shortcomings, we have learned how to transmute those actions and shortcomings into something useful for all concerned, including ourselves. Some of us, on the other hand, are forced to wear a yoke of disgrace, simply because fate has decreed no clever escapes this time round, and as a result of not having learned to turn that yoke into the mantle of a king, a yoke it remains. Yet, the bottom line is that none of us are any less guilty than anyone else, and neither are any of us more guilty than anyone else. All of us participate in the process of life, and because of that participation none of us can plead innocence. For example, if I buy a car and run somebody down with it, then it is undeniably true that I am guilty of that person's injury. But had there been no cars to buy, I would only have been able to knock that person over with, let us say, my bicycle, in which case the injury to him would more than likely have been considerably less. Therefore, indirectly, everyone involved in the automobile industry is responsible every time someone on the roads is injured or killed as a result of a car accident.

By the example above I am not trying to pass the buck, I am simply pointing out that if I run someone down with my car, then although I must own and take responsibility for that act, nevertheless I could never have been guilty of that crime had some other person not invented cars, had some other person not started to manufacture cars, had some others not started to sell cars, and had yet others still not encouraged people to buy cars by arranging the necessary finances for those who would otherwise not be able to afford cars. At the end of the day, there is only one life and one humanity and a destiny which is common to all. By owning our actions and our experiences, we take ownership of the knowledge gained, and with that knowledge we all play our part in creating the world we live in.

WHAT IS LIFE?

Our wishes are not just idle day-dreams. Our wishes are an expression of our innermost predilection — a predilection which it is perfectly possible to fulfil, provided we use our knowledge wisely.

What is life? I like to look at life as a huge web. In this web the actions of every individual are the many threads or strands which criss-cross each other in making up that web. Each thread is interdependent upon and interacts with all the other threads, and so the whole web of life is thoroughly and completely interrelated. We can therefore say that life resembles a sphere of relationships, encompassing not only other people, but also animals, plants and even inanimate objects such as the furniture in our homes. Think for a moment about the relationship you have with the furniture in your home. Think, for example, about the cupboards which have doors that always glide open with the greatest of ease and those cupboards with which you always have to struggle until finally the door swings open with such force as to knock you on the nose or the shin. Your relationships with all the people in your life are no different, and the same applies to your relationships with the circumstances in your life.

All of our lives are nothing more than a set of relationships between us and the circumstances in our lives. These circumstances are not just of our own making, since any circumstance in life is dependent upon the relationship between us and, at the very least, one more person or thing, such as a cupboard door. Therefore, if you are in search of happiness, the issue which has to be addressed is relationships, but I wonder if you have ever thought what a huge undertaking this really is?

Relationships form the very essence of life, for life is indeed one big web of energy fields which are all interactive, interdependent and interrelated. We term this web the circle of beingness, for life is not open-ended, but is curved back upon itself to form a closed circle or, more accurately, a closed sphere.

To learn about relationships is to learn about life itself. Consequently, if you wish to relate in a happy and meaningful way to another person, to the world around you and, most important of all, to yourself, you will need to reassess everything you have been taught about relationships and, in fact, to re-evaluate everything you think you know about people and the world we live in.

I am therefore going to ask you to join me in a little game — a game of life. This game is known as the Journey of Adjustment.

This game begins with the plot of a story — a story about you and me — a story which will unfold progressively during the course of this book and which will come to its conclusion once you have grasped wherein lies the key to happiness.

We did not invent this game, for life itself gives us the plot. But in case you have missed it somewhere along the line, I will give you the plot. Remember though, that this plot is only the bare bones of what will become the story of your life. You, and you alone, determine the details of the story, the characters that are or will be featuring in it, and whether or not it is to be a tragedy, a comedy, an epic drama or simply a poignant tale of the life, the challenges and the predilection of one man or one woman, namely you, who is in search of happiness, joy and freedom.

We make of our lives what we will.

TWO

THE JOURNEY OF ADJUSTMENT & THE 4 TERMS OF CAPTAIN LIFE

*You live on an island. This island is your world,
and on it you have everything you need.*

The island you live on is nice enough, except that it does feel very much like an island, in that although you are surrounded by a great many other islands, you often feel isolated and cut off, with the result that you are alone with only your own thoughts, feelings and emotions. Loneliness is the name you give your island and you long to get to know the rest of the world.

Then one day a ship comes to dock at your island. Excited, you run down to the shore to meet the ship, and you find standing on the deck a very impressive-looking man whom you assume to be the captain.

You are so excited that you hardly greet the man before begging him to grant you passage aboard his ship. With much gesticulating you explain to him how lonely you are, that you want to get off your island and that you would like to get to know the rest of the world.

Whilst you are talking, the captain of the ship stands quietly, listening attentively to your tale, and even for some time after you have finished speaking he still observes you silently. Finally, just as you are about to ask him once more for passage, the man starts to speak.

"I am Captain Life", he says, "And I am indeed Captain of this ship. But I must warn you that my ship is no ordinary ship, for it is the Ship of Adjustment. If you wish to have passage aboard my ship, it shall be granted, but only on the terms I shall set."

"Yes!" you reply eagerly. "Oh, yes! I will do anything that you command, and I will pay you any fee you ask for."

Again the man looks at you for a long while in silence before replying.

"I charge no fee for passage, for if I were to charge you for travelling aboard the Ship of Adjustment, you would never be able to afford the passage. But these are my terms.

"Firstly, when you come aboard my ship you may not bring with you any books, or photographs, or paintings. Instead you will bring only a pen and blank paper. Secondly, you must not bring with you any clothing or shoes of any description, but you may clothe yourself in only a white cotton sheet. Thirdly, you may wear no jewellery or weapons upon your person — only a laurel crown and a garland of wild flowers. Fourthly, you must cast your watch into the sea. And finally, before you will be allowed to leave my ship, you will be required to give me a special password which you will have to try and learn whilst taking passage aboard the Ship of Adjustment. Should you try to cheat in any way whatsoever, or fail to give the correct password at the end of your journey, you will forfeit your life."

Such is the plot of our story, the story of you and me, the story of you and someone else, the story of you and many others, the story of you and the world out there and, most important of all, the story of you and your own inner self.

Welcome aboard the Ship of Adjustment, but see to it that you pay the most careful attention to the terms of Captain Life, for we can forfeit our lives in many different ways, not necessarily only through physical death. Therefore let us consider each of Captain Life's terms, one by one, but since this is to be your story, I cannot give you the answers, simply because my answers are right only for me, and so they will not necessarily be right for you.

Each of us must find out for ourselves what the terms laid down by Captain Life really mean, and how best we as individuals must adjust in order to meet those terms. However, the password we are required to learn during our passage through life is the same for all of us. So, bon voyage! Enjoy the journey!

THREE

TERM 1:
BECOMING AWARE OF ANOTHER'S STATE OF BEING

Life is not your social conditioning.

Let us consider the first of Captain Life's terms, namely, "When you come aboard my ship you may not bring with you any books, or photographs, or paintings. Instead you will bring only a pen and blank paper."

The implications are that if we wish to participate in life, rather than in social conditioning, then we need to forget everything we have been taught (books), and we must discard everything we think we know (photographs and paintings), so that we can start writing a new script (pen and blank paper) for the life we would like to have.

Think for a moment about what you have been taught. Were you ever taught to think for yourself? Or were you merely taught to think like everybody else? Were you ever given the tools with which to find the meaning of life for yourself? Or were you merely instructed in upholding the prejudices and beliefs of others? Were you ever taught to value your own experience over and above information gained from others? Or were you mostly reprimanded into feeling embarrassed by your experiences? What have you learned that you can truly call your own knowledge? In fact, if you really want to be honest, you will be horrified to realise how little of what you profess to know is your own knowledge gained through your own experience. Most of the stuff people look upon as their knowledge is in fact only the ideas and beliefs of others, often untried and untested as to their validity and efficacy, and which have been assimilated through either voluntary or enforced social conditioning.

If then you have so little real knowledge about life or, more precisely, since you have placed so little value upon what you yourself have learned through practical experience, is it surprising that you should find it difficult to relate to others, to life and, above all, to yourself? But let us take a closer look at what all of this really means.

It doesn't matter who we are trying to relate to, whether this is our romantic partner, our parents, our siblings, our employer or the world in general; if we are to relate properly to others the first step is for us take the other person's state of being into consideration, and this is true also in relating to ourselves. Yet how aware are you of your own state of being, let alone that of others? By "state of being", I mean where any person, including you, is at in his or her life — how that person thinks, feels and responds because of the circumstances in his or her life.

In order to see how rarely we are aware of another's, or our own, state of being we only need to look at the many different types of relationship in the world around us. For example, all too often amongst siblings we find that even though they mostly share a common view of the world, they very rarely, if ever, share a common dream. The only things most siblings have in common are their parents, for instead of really relating to each other, in the sense of taking each other's state of being into consideration, there is often only a sense of rivalry — a sense of "if you hadn't been born, then I could have had all the attention." Such a relationship can hardly be termed "relating to", but is rather more in the nature of competition which has its basis in the feeling of being threatened in some way. As a result, siblings tend to spend more time in competing against each other for their parents' attention, or in trying to outdo each other academically, or on the sports field, than in trying to get to know each other.

Even in the workplace we find this same sense of competing against others, rather than a striving together in an endeavour to complement one another, by getting to know both the strengths and the weaknesses in ourselves and our colleagues. Consequently, colleagues in the workplace tend mostly to be unspoken enemies, each being terrified that someone in the office will actually get to know them for who and what they really are. But once again, it is very difficult to relate to a facade, to an act; we can only relate successfully with the real person behind the mask.

The examples can go on and on. How often do a mother and daughter not go into undeclared competition for the father's attention, simply because neither of them truly believe in their own value and therefore need a man's assurance in order to feel better about themselves? How often does a son not try desperately to live up to his father's expectations of him, believing that unless he does so his father will not love him for being just who and what he is? How often does a mother not run her son's life even long after he has left home, simply because he does not trust his own knowledge, and because his mother cannot find any value in her own life unless she is needed by her son? How often does an employer not resort to enforcing authoritarianism rather than practising participative management, and simply because he has such a low self-esteem that he feels threatened by even the tea girl?

We can make our list as long as we like, but if you will look into your own life, you will see your own examples of competition versus relationship. Irrespective of all outer appearances, the bottom line in all these cases is, firstly, not taking into consideration the other person's state of being; and secondly, not believing in your own knowledge and value, and therefore feeling threatened by all and sundry. With this in mind, one can see that very few people have relationships in the true sense of the word, for instead of relating to others, they are merely competing against those people, the end result of which is a behaviour pattern which is normally quite destructive to all parties concerned. In this respect, realise that the fruit of any true relationship is both uplifting and strengthening to both parties. This follows from the meaning of the word, which is, "to connect to" or "to connect with", and which, of course, is the very antithesis of "competing against".

As an exercise to see how well you rate in your supposed relationships, make a list of them all, giving special attention to those relationships which are so often taken for granted, for example, your relationship with your neighbours, your weekly maid, your household pet and most especially your relationship with yourself. In doing this, do not try to kid yourself, for it is total honesty that is called for here, and it is therefore important that you pay careful attention to even those relationships which you think are good, remembering in respect of these that the mark of a true relationship is one which is mutually uplifting and strengthening, and not one which is mutually destructive and weakening. For example, look at your friends, and assess for yourself whether you and your friends support each other in your strengths, or whether you merely commiserate with each other in your weaknesses. A true friend is someone who loves you enough to speak his or her mind openly and without fear of losing the friendship for having spoken up. Someone who agrees with even your most unimpeccable actions and behaviour simply so as to keep the friendship is not a friend, but rather a partner in crime!

USING FEAR

*To relate to ourselves, to others, or to the world,
we need to be aware.*

The first step in starting to relate properly is to cultivate the habit of being fully alert to everything around you, as well as inside of you. Being alert is not only a prerequisite for being aware of another's state of being, but it is also vital for cultivating a fluidity in our perception. In other words, it will not help you to go through life fixated upon only your own point of view. Instead you need to develop an openness to all points of view, but without doubting your own knowledge when you do so. You will soon find as many different points of view as there are people in the world. This should hardly be surprising considering that each individual is unique in his or her approach to life. But the real beauty in all of this is that each person's point of view is like one facet of a diamond. Therefore you have one facet, I have another, and yet others have completely different facets, but when we put all of those facets together, what a brilliance of light is reflected by that diamond. What a magnificent intelligence is displayed when many minds join forces in one endeavour, instead of competing against each other in the sense of "I'm right and therefore you must be wrong." To develop this kind of approach to life is a benefit of being aware.

TERM 1: BECOMING AWARE OF ANOTHER'S STATE OF BEING

With respect to the word "awareness", you should remember to differentiate clearly between awareness and consciousness. The word consciousness means to "share knowledge", which, of course, implies taking into account another person's state of being. Awareness, on the other hand, means "the quality or condition of being emotionally and intuitively sensitive", but more significantly, has its origins in the Latin word "vereri", meaning "to be fearful".

This is relevant in our consideration of relationships, for wherever there is fear, or even just a sense of fear, the person concerned will be hyper-alert and therefore wide awake. However, in speaking about "a sense of fear" as opposed to plain "fear", we are once again carefully differentiating between two very different states of being. An analogy may help to clarify this.

Think of a fire, and what happens when you hold your hand close to that fire. Normally you will experience a sense of burning, and that sense of burning will bring up in you a sense of fear that will stop you from being stupid enough to plunge your hand into red hot coals. If, on the other hand, someone has you all trussed up like a bundle and is busy rolling you towards a nice big fire, you will not just be sensing a fear of burning, but will more than likely already be in a total panic in anticipation of being used for a taper!

This distinction is so important because most people will only ever become wide awake, or fully aware, when their survival is being threatened in some way. Therefore it is always either real fear, or at least the sense of fear, that spurs people into a state of wakefulness, or awareness. However, since we are trying to learn to relate, rather than constantly feeling threatened by even a firefly, we cannot afford to have ourselves forced into being aware. We need to develop this faculty consciously. The main reason for this is that unless their physical survival is being threatened, most people simply succumb to their fear, in the sense of being so caught up in it that they are debilitated by it.

To be debilitated by fear is a very common occurrence, and the effects are the same for everyone — you become drained of your strength and you feel weak and powerless. In short, as your fear grows, so your strength goes.

People all too often feel bad about admitting to their fear. We get taught that it is a sign of weakness, or some such deficiency. Yet this need not be and should not be. All of the evolution of life on this planet takes place through the medium of fear, for all types of fear are merely so many different expressions of the instinct to self-preservation. All plants, animals, insects and human beings register fear. Look around you and see if there is anything at all that is not subject to fear.

And yet, although it is experienced by all life-forms, fear is a strangely intangible force, an emotion which we cannot ever fully identify, although clearly we need to bring it into its proper perspective if it is not going to debilitate us. Therefore let us consider an example of how fear can debilitate us.

Consider the insurance companies. These companies dominate our economy, for they are some of the biggest economic powers. Why? Because all of their business is based upon the element of fear. If you let an insurance agent into your home, the chances are that by the time he leaves you will have invested in insurance against fire, insurance against theft, insurance against medical expenses and, to boot, a life insurance. And all of this investment will be purely because the agent will have earned himself a fat commission on having instilled in you a very real fear that unless you have all of these insurances, you will be in dire straits when, (note, not if), all these catastrophies strike you. The fact that you might well be a single person, but that you have still ended up being insured against kicking the bucket, even though you have neither spouse, child, relative, dog, cat, or parrot, may well puzzle you for some time to come, or at least for as long as it takes for you to become aware that you have been ripped off, but the fear will most certainly be quite pervasive!

However, on a more positive note, remember that it is also fear which drives us, spurs us on to becoming bigger and better, wiser and more tolerant, more awake and therefore also more responsive. Consequently, to be fully aware and wide awake, we need to be fearful in the sense of, "I'm afraid this insurance agent is going to try to force me into parting with a considerable portion of my income". Obviously this is an altogether different ball-game to being debilitated by fear in the sense of, "Oh, dear! I fear the consequences to myself if I do not follow the advice of this insurance agent."

Therefore in being wide awake we need, first of all, to acknowledge our fear, instead of trying to pretend it is not there, or trying to brush it aside; and secondly, to face our fear and get it into its proper perspective, so that we can learn to use it to our advantage rather than allowing it to debilitate us.

DEVELOPING RESPECT

*Being wide awake implies not only using your fear,
but also developing respect.*

Through being wide awake we learn to use our fear in the manner of a tool with which to keep us on our toes. However, if we are to learn to use fear constructively we also need to know the meaning of respect, not only for others but also for ourselves. Where there is no sense of fear we will too quickly start taking things, or people, for granted. Realise, though, that to spend one's life half asleep, and not to have any sense of fear, implies a flippant attitude towards life — an attitude that smacks of not caring either about oneself or others. Such an attitude is very much a case of "If you don't like it, lump it," and "If I lose this relationship, or this house, there are plenty more fish in the sea, and plenty more houses on the market". Such an attitude is one of total disrespect.

Therefore the real meaning of being wide awake is to have a sense of fear based upon respect. Where there is no fear and no respect you will soon find yourself nodding off, since you are bored out of your mind, and if you are not in your mind, then you cannot possibly be awake!

Putting all of this into a nutshell: if by now you have figured out that your relationships are working at a mere 10%, it means that you are snoring for 90% of the time.

If, on the other hand, you have no idea what I'm on about, I don't blame you. It also took me an awfully long time to figure out why all my most treasured relationships always mysteriously ended up as a soggy gooey mess. You know the kind of relationship I mean? Those nice, warm, comfortable ones in which one lies around and shares even one's darkest secrets until all hours of the morning. I always wondered why those relationships so quickly ended up in mutual contempt, until finally it dawned on me that what was missing in all of these relationships was fear and respect.

Practically speaking, what does this really mean? In order to see this in action, let's take the example of a romantic relationship.

Consider any young man who has met a gorgeous girl a few days before. Now Tom has not been able to stop thinking about the pretty Thea ever since he met her, and having finally come to the momentous conclusion that he simply must see her again, Tom has the thoroughly original idea of phoning Thea to ask her out to dinner. But this is now where the sense of fear can begin to surface.

Suddenly Tom is no longer so sure about himself, and as a result all sorts of fears begin to shake his belief in himself. "What happens if she does not want to go out with me?" "What happens if I find out that she is married, or engaged, or something like that?" "What will I do if she tells me straight out that she thinks I'm a jerk?"

Needless to say, we all know how Tom is going to handle that first date if he does scrape his courage together and manages to invite Thea to dinner. Tom will be wide awake, and oh, so very attentive! He will be aware of his every move, his every smile, his every wink, and he will not miss even the slightest opportunity of making Thea feel like a virgin queen. Even before Tom leaves the house he will make doubly certain that he looks at his best and most masculine. The car will be washed and polished, the house tiptop for coffee after the meal, and his aftershave will still be heavy in the air from the night before when the bouquet of flowers arrives at Thea's front door the following morning.

But now, what happens? Thea has fallen hopelessly in love with this dashing and utterly charming young prince, and consequently marries him on the turn with stars in her eyes —stars that quickly enough turn into daggers, for now having made his catch, good old Tom is once again back to his usual self. Sloppy old jeans and dirty t-shirt, dried out shaving cream lying in the bathroom which is littered with his clothing from the day before. Tom is sprawled out on the couch in the TV room watching soccer, or some other equally vile sport, whilst Thea is doing the cooking, the laundry, struggling with a lawnmower that is too big for her, and trying to wash the car in the hot afternoon sun.

"Flowers? You want, flowers, my dear Thea? Why? If you would like flowers go pick them. I see you have planted a whole garden full of them."

Get the picture? Respect has flown out the window because Tom no longer feels the need to be fearful. After all, he is quite the hottest hunk around the neighbourhood, and although he may not be too macho with the lawnmower, he knows how to make the bed rattle and squeak. Thea should be only too grateful that he, Tom, chose her for his wife! In his complacency, Tom is not even aware of the fact that Thea's adoring smile has become one of open contempt.

We find exactly the same principle operating within our work environment. For example, your boss suddenly informs you that he would like to have a meeting with you at 14h00 sharp, but doesn't tell you what the meeting is going to be about. In that moment up comes the sense of fear again, especially if, for example, you have not been able to finish your latest project on time. All sorts of thoughts and questions based upon fear will start going through your mind. "Gee! Am I going to be fired?" "Am I going to be reprimanded?" "Am I going to lose my bonus?" "What's actually going to happen in that meeting?"

But once again that sense of fear, that sense of the unknown, will make you wide awake and will also make you far more respectful than you would normally be. So, by the time you walk into that office at 14h00, not knowing what to expect, you are going to be very respectful, very much on your toes and certainly very wide awake.

Therefore if you want any relationship to be successful and fulfilling, you need to remain wide awake, and in order to do that you cannot ever afford to become complacent by forgetting your fear, neither can you ever afford not to be utterly respectful.

THE DIFFERENCES BETWEEN MALE AND FEMALE

> *Life revolves around polarities, whether negative and positive, black and white, spirit and man or male and female.*

Having looked at the example of Tom and Thea, we now come to that age-old thorny issue surrounding the true role of the male and the female. What do you understand of this concept? Or have you long since abandoned all hope of ever understanding it and submitted to utter confusion?

Here is where you are really going to have to put aside all of your social conditioning, or at least for long enough to hear me out. If you will only bear with me, you might find that you end up liking what I have to say!

Nonetheless, it is not your blind trust that I am asking for. What I am suggesting is that once you have an overall picture of what I am trying to get across, you can at least try this section out for yourself. If it works for you, then that will be great, but it is senseless to discard something when you don't even know what it is, or before at least trying it out as to its usefulness.

Even if you have put these techniques into practice, and you find that they are not working for you, then first of all check whether you have applied them correctly. If you haven't, then apply them correctly and see if they now work for you. If, after you are totally certain that you are applying the techniques correctly, they still do not work for you, then by all means chuck this book out the window!

What are the basic differences between the male and the female? The way in which things have been set up by the powers of nature is that the male is the hunter. Therefore, it is the male who goes out to the workplace, and it is primarily he who must bring home the food.

The female, on the other hand, because she holds within herself the mysteries of conception and childbirth, is the one who stays at home tending the hearth and the family.

In later books in this series we will be looking at all of this in much greater detail, but for now I am just introducing this all-important concept so that this section makes more sense.

But what does this actually mean? Quite simply, it means that the male, because it is he who carries and secretes the life-giving sperm, is predominantly concerned with the world around him, that is, with the outer world. Just as his reproductive organs are situated on the outside of his body, so too does the male secrete his sperm into the outside world. In other words, in the same way that the male must plant the fields surrounding his home so as to propagate food, so must he also find a wife in whom to plant his sperm if he is to propagate his species. This means that the male instinctively regards himself as being a part of the greater world, and knows that if he is going to be able to grow his crops and find a wife, then he needs to be in harmony with the world around him. In this respect, realise that for the male it is ultimately only him and the world out there, and that his survival, as well as that of his family, is very much dependent upon his harmonious interaction with that big, bad world out there. Therefore it is one thing to be all cocky with your neighbour when you are on the safe side of the fence, but discretion is by far the better part of valour when your opponent in business is very clearly busy manoeuvring himself into a position of gaining the upper hand! Likewise, to be the hunter stalking a buck is quite exciting, but to be stalked by a hungry lion is not nearly as much fun, and unless the hunter is intimately familiar with the world around him, which he can only be if he is in harmony with it, the lion will not be hungry for long.

The female, because she is tending the hearth and the family, is not concerned with the world out there, for in the same way that her reproductive organs are situated on the inside of her body, so too does conception and pregnancy take place on the inside of the female's body. Therefore, being essentially concerned with caring for the unborn child in her womb, just as she is in caring for the born children left in her care in the cave which is her family's home, the female is essentially cut off from the outer world. As a result, the female automatically delves within herself to find answers to how best, let us say, raise her children, and how to keep the cave clean and warm, for, to the female, her outer cave is highly symbolic of her inner cave, that is, her womb. Thus the woman instinctively knows she has to turn within, and so she is far more concerned with the inner world than with the outer world.

The main difference which emerges here is that the male has to practise harmony in order to be a successful hunter, whereas the female, through having to delve within herself to find the answers she seeks, becomes more and more engrossed in analysing and dividing in order to achieve clarity on any specific problem.

The overall effect of these most basic differences is that the male learns to think in order to outwit his prey, and to discover where best to plant his seed, whilst the female, through having to ascertain what is happening within the cave of her home, as well as within the cave of her womb, learns to rely more upon gut feeling, that is, feeling with the womb.

USING YOUR OWN KNOWLEDGE

True thinking has nothing to do with internal dialogue.

It is quite sad that although we are all encouraged to rationalise, no-one actually teaches us to think in the true sense of the word. We are all experts at juggling concepts around in our minds — concepts which invariably bring forth all sorts of emotions, and these spark off even more ideas or concepts, which in turn also bring forth more emotions. Thus there is seldom any real thought, only what we term internal dialogue.

If you want to be honest with yourself, how often do you really think "straight"? You know, like right now?

"Why is he asking me that question? (Growl!) Who gives him the right to infer that I can't think straight? It is just like that man the other day who was implying that I was trying to do him in just because I had not paid my bill on time. Oh, heavens! (Panic) That reminds me! I think I forgot to tell the kids that I will be late picking them up from school today. (Perplexed as to what to do. Anxiety) Can't think straight! Bah! (Indignation) Arrogant arsehole! Shall I phone the school to contact the kids? (Discomfort) What on earth will the school secretary think of me? (Annoyance and frustration) Oh, damned! Can't think straight! Maybe I should......?"

Does this somehow ring a bell with you? That is what

we call internal dialogue, as opposed to true thinking, which never takes any time to perform and is always clean and clear because it is the instantaneous recall or registration of knowledge. However, in order to understand what this actually means, you should know that there is a huge difference between real knowledge and information.

Information is exactly what the word implies — information about something we have not known before, and invariably gained through some outside source, such as another person, a book, the radio, television, etcetera. Knowledge, on the other hand, arises from within, in that it is something you know for sure either because you have experienced it in the past, or else because you are experiencing it right now. For example, if you have never been to France, but you are reading literature on France, you are gaining outside information on France. But if you arrive in France, and are travelling through that country, you are gaining firsthand personal experience of that country.

It does not matter how much literature you have read on France, and it does not matter how many people you have spoken to who have been to France, for until you yourself have been to France you cannot claim to have knowledge of France in the true sense of the word. Therefore France to you remains the unknown, about which you may or may not have some information. Once you have firsthand experience of France, though, you can rightfully claim to know

France, or to have knowledge of France, in which case that country is now for you the known.

Now in coming back to our consideration of the male and the female, the reason why it is so important to know the difference between knowledge or experience, as opposed to information, is that if we are to define the true roles of the male and the female accurately, we need to grasp what is meant by the known and the unknown.

If we look at the male, who is the hunter, we see that he can only hunt his prey with the knowledge which is available to him. In other words, since he has to recall and draw on what is known to him, the male is predominantly occupied with the known. The male may well also experiment with information he has gleaned from somewhere else, but until he has tried out that information he cannot know if or how it works.

The female, because she is constantly having to delve within herself to come up with answers to her challenges, is constantly facing the unknown, that is, the unknown within herself. Herein lies the female's real challenge, for unlike the male, who is concerned with making his mark in the outside world with what for him is the known, the female has to find answers to what is not known, and in order to do this, she delves into the unknown of her own inner being. What this implies is that in dealing with the unknown, there is nothing to think about, simply because there is no previous knowledge to recall. Therefore, when the female delves into the unknown, it means that she is up against a challenge that she has not experienced before and, as a result, she is quite literally pioneering in the true sense of the word. But as always in pioneering, the only thing the female can really rely upon is her feeling, that is, feeling her way in the dark — feeling her way within the dark of the unknown.

This should not be taken as suggesting that the female does not think, or that the male does not feel. I am simply pointing out here the basic differences in approach between the true male and the true female. There are a great many times when the male is called upon to feel, but even when this does happen, the male will still have a predilection for thinking, in the sense of comparing his feeling with that which is known. Likewise, the female will often act upon the known, but here too, because she is predominantly occupied with the inner world, she will more often than not sense that her knowledge of any given situation is not enough to provide all the answers that she feels are needed. Consequently, even in thinking about the situation, and even in recalling her knowledge, she will have a predilection for instinctively feeling into the unknown.

FEELINGS AND EMOTIONS ARE NOT THE SAME

Emotion will always guide you to true feeling.

If feeling is best described as intuition, or sensing, or quite simply, gut feel, emotion is something we are all fully familiar with. Strangely enough, there is essentially only one emotion, namely, desire. Desire can be expressed by the words "I want to", which is a basic verbalisation of emotion. Nevertheless, desire does have four aspects: fear, anger, melancholy and joy. Fear is the desire to retreat, anger is the desire to fight, melancholy, the desire to change, and joy, the desire for life. Just a little thought on each of these definitions will soon make their deeper meanings clear.

If we look at all this in relation to the roles of the true male and the true female, we see that again there is a difference in approach, although not in usage. In the male's case it is him and the world out there, and therefore he tends to have a predilection for thinking. For the female it's her and her inner world, with the result that she relies far more upon feeling and, in this, learns also to work with the emotions far more consciously than the male.

For example, John and Barbara have an argument about something and both become angry, or both call forth the desire to fight. At first they fight each other, Barbara screaming at John that she feels he is not being caring enough, whilst John retorts angrily that he thinks she is being totally unreason-able. John, of course, has reached for the sword of the known and, since he cannot recall any knowledge of where he has been uncaring, demands that Barbara gives him an example. She, on the other hand, cannot come up with any definite examples that make reason-able sense to John, simply because she is all fired-up with feeling, and is therefore brandishing around the sword of the unknown!

I am sure you have had dozens of such experiences. Barbara is acting upon the unknown, a hunch, a feeling, but John wants an answer based upon the known, and since she is unable to give him a reason-able answer, that is, an answer about which he can reason, he storms out of the house thinking that his wife is mad.

Barbara, left alone at home to look after the kids, the dog, the parrot, the ironing, the cooking and the garden, has no other recourse but to allow her anger, (her emotion), to guide her into finding the answers she seeks. Determined to find the answers to her feeling that her husband is not caring enough, she uses her anger to explore the depths of her own inner unknown.

John, on the other hand, is halfway down the road, using his anger, (his emotion), to guide him into trying to think about his wife's madness, but after not being able to find reasonable answers to his questions, unconsciously starts to get a *feeling* for what perhaps his wife was trying to tell him. Having got that feeling, John stops dead in his tracks and starts applying what he has just sensed, by means of comparing it with what it is he already knows about his behaviour.

However, in both instances, we see how emotion will always guide us into feeling our way around in the dark — if we only allow this most natural process to take place. But sadly, most of the time this process is ignored. Therefore instead of allowing his anger to guide him to a feeling, John will simply hit the pub with a vengeance, in the hope of finding a partner in crime who will commiserate with him on the unreasonableness of females. Back home, Barbara, instead of allowing her anger to guide her into a deeper feeling, will more often than not also find a partner in crime, or else will resort to feeling bad about herself, in the sense of feeling that she is too stupid to speak to her husband intelligently.

Yet all of this heartache is so unnecessary, if only both men and women will pause to consider that just as their bodies are different, so too are their respective functions different, and therefore also so too must their approach to life be different. In the next section we will look at the how these differences are meant to be reconciled, and how a man and a woman˙ can co-operate intelligently with each other, instead of going at each other with two swords which are, by definition, mutually incompatible.

TERM 1: BECOMING AWARE OF ANOTHER'S STATE OF BEING

WHAT IS TRUE LOVE?

The cornerstone of true love is intelligent co-operation.

To love your spouse, your child, your boss, or your parrot to bits, is no guarantee that your spouse will remain devoted to you forever, that your child will not defy your well-meant guidance, that your boss will not suddenly retrench you, or that your parrot will not bite your hand when you try to clean his cage. Most people's understanding of the word love has nothing at all to do with intelligent co-operation. In fact, the word "love", as well as the bizarre family of feelings that are normally associated with it, is today so widely de-fined, that it has no definition left! Having become defined to the nth degree, it is nothing but an unintelligible justification for all manner of vices, prejudices and preconceived ideas which make up the biggest portion of people's baggage — baggage which is mostly so coarse and so gross in content, that there is nothing fine about it. But what is even worse, is that it is all this de-fined baggage which people hang around the necks of their beloved ones, and woe to him or her who should even contemplate rejecting such an un-fine yoke! A yoke is not love. A yoke is a yoke, no matter how much we try to justify our attempts at enslaving another being.

True love, on the other hand, is a very fine thing indeed, and just because it is so very fine, cannot be de-fined in terms of words. True love can only be shown in terms of action. Thus, we demonstrate our love through our actions towards another, rather than demanding that the other person should live up to the set of conditions most people define as constituting love. You know what I mean. "If you love me, then you will fetch me my slippers." "If you love me, then you will not shout at me." "If you love me, you will give me more pocket money, and will never say no whenever I want to stay over at a friend's house." "If you love me, you will not encourage your secretary to sit on your lap." "If you love me, you will do this, you will do that, you mustn't do this, you mustn't do that." And so the list goes on and on, and the real meaning of the word becomes ever more distorted.

Demonstrating our love has nothing to do with fetching slippers or with handing out more pocket money. Demonstrating love means demonstrating intelligence within the act of co-operation. "Let me fetch you your slippers whilst you light the fire, because that way we save time — time we can spend together." "I will gladly pay you for mowing the lawn, in which case you can earn more pocket money, and I save by not having to use the gardening services." True love means sharing in the responsibility of co-creating the circumstances we wish for in our lives — circumstances that bring about feelings of trust, of belief in one another, of safeness and, above all, of warmth. Because true love is unconditional, it can only come into being when two people are prepared to co-operate intelligently towards building a relationship that is based, not upon expectations, (which are seldom, if ever fulfilled), but upon mutual respect, camaraderie, and that genuine warmth which comes from knowing that "If you win, then so do I", rather than, "Why don't you help me win this victory over you."

Where there is intelligent co-operation, true unconditional love is the inevitable result, a result that does not need to be defined, simply because the actions, or the inter-actions between the two people concerned, speak for themselves.

In order to understand how best to accomplish intelligent co-operation, we need to look closely at all of the social conditioning that we have gathered concerning both males and females, and especially within the context of romantic relationships. Therefore, think of everything you have been taught and everything you believe you have learned concerning both men and women. Now consider for a moment; how much of what you know tells you anything about how men and women are supposed to relate, that is, to co-operate intelligently? Yet realise that if the information you have is correct, then that information should make it quite clear how intelligent co-operation is to be achieved.

But the simple truth of the matter is that none of us have ever been taught what it really means to be a male or a female, and much less what is entailed in the act of intelligent co-operation. What's more, very few people in the world today realise that both men and women are essentially hermaphroditic, in that all men have an inner female side, just as all women have an inner male side.

Our physical bodies, and the sexual differences in our bodies, are simply a physical expression of the approach we are meant to take in this particular lifetime towards the evolution of our awareness. So if you have a male body, then on goes the thinking cap, and out into the big bad world you march with the banner of reason held high. But if you have a female body, then out comes the handkerchief to wipe away a tear or two, as you wave your man on his way, and before going back into your cave, your womb, your feelings. And yet, even as a man, you too have an inner cave — the ability to feel and to sense from the gut; just as the female too has an inner banner of reason which guides her through the darkness of the unknown, the endless labyrinths of human feeling. Realise though, that the gut is not the same as the womb, and neither is female reason the logic of male reason. For the male, feeling is inherent, a primordial knowing that he is here and that he needs to go there, and therefore his reason is linear in quality and consequently logical. For the female, feeling is all-pervasive, an evolving, or unfolding knowing that she is not going anywhere because she needs to be right here, and therefore is her reason circular in quality and more in the nature of gathering together all the bits and pieces that are required for being here now.

UNDERSTANDING MIRRORS

You are not your behaviour.

However, if we are to understand all of this mystical stuff, then it is vital for us to accept that we are mysterious creatures and that we have sides to our natures which we cannot see ourselves. People time and time again make the fatal mistake of assuming that they know themselves, when in actual fact the only thing they do know about themselves is how their behaviour is affected by the actions of others. Therefore it is with much presumed rather than true wisdom that someone says: "I know myself, for if you step on my toes, I know I will slap you; and if you steal my wife I know I shall wring your neck; and if you buy me an ice-cream, then, that is so kind of you, but what in hell's name is your ulterior motive for doing so?" Yet, what do any of these reactions to the actions of others tell us about who and what we really are? For example, if I change the gears in my car, the car reacts in a certain way, and if you try to change my point of view, then I too react in a certain way. But having noted the reactions of both my car and myself, this still does not make me understand how a car really works, or how someone can manage to make me react happily, sadly, angrily, or just plain stupidly. The only thing most people ever really learn from all of this wise observation is that my car is a lot less stubborn in having its gears shifted than I am in having my point of view shifted! Generally, people only ever learn to play the blame game. "How can you be so stubborn?" "I am not stubborn. You are the one who is stubborn!" Does this sound familiar?

However, it is not the fact that people play the blame game that is the problem, it is the fact that people never come to realise that the people around us are only our mirrors. Get the picture? So there you are standing in your bathroom in front of the mirror shaving, whilst all the time fuming about your stubborn wife, or kids, or dog, or boss. But the person you are conversing with in the mirror is you! In other words, if you are stubborn, your mirrors are forced to reflect that stubbornness for you. But if you are open-minded, then your mirrors must likewise reflect that openness for you. Therefore there is nothing wrong with playing the blame game, as long as we remember that if we do not like the face we are seeing in the mirror, then it is not the mirror's fault, or God's fault, but your own fault for having such an ugly face!

The concept of mirrors is not just restricted to our behaviour, but is equally applicable to our actions. Therefore if you steal the odd bit of stationary from work, or you "think" that no-one will mind if you take off from work for a little longer at lunchtime, then don't become indignant when one of your kids filches a few coins from your wallet, or a passing tramp "thinks" that you would not miss a couple of items off your washing line. What goes round comes round, and mirrors have a very inconsiderate tendency to reflect.

People are oblivious to the existence of mirrors, for the simple reason that they generally speaking only like nice mirrors, mirrors that show only the pretty side. "Oh! What an utterly adorable little girl. She reminds me so much of what I was like when I was that age. Such pretty rosy cheeks. Such beautiful hair. Such a loving smile." "Oh! What a perfectly horrid child! She reminds me so much of you when you sulk. Such an ugly scowl! Why don't you teach your child some manners!" I think you see my point, but if you would like to have more technical information on the true nature of mirrors, then you will have to read my other books.

The most important aspect about mirrors is that we cannot see our own inner selves, or our behaviour, without some kind of a mirror. This is especially true if we are trying to grasp our inner other half. Both males and females need to have a relationship with a member of the opposite sex in order to come to grips with their own inner counterhalf. It is only by studying the females around him that a man comes to understand the differences between males and females and, in that process, not only comes to understand his own inner female, but also begins to grasp what it is to be a true male. It is simply not possible to learn what it is to be a male when one is surrounded only by men who are just as ignorant and bewildered as you as to what it means to be a male. The only thing you will learn from other men is to take your drink standing up, to walk and talk like a real macho and to brag about your sexual prowess. In short, the only thing you will learn from your own sex is even more social conditioning. But the moment your wife locks you out for having come home drunk, or tries to stifle a giggle when you have just puffed out your manly chest, or turns her back to you in bed because she has a "headache", you are forced either into playing the blame game, or into doing some real deep soul-searching. Needless to say, although I have in this example used the masculine gender, exactly the same goes for the female.

The bottom line in all of this is that males and females are equal but different. Therefore, instead of engaging in the battle of the sexes and in blaming each other, we must study our counterparts in order to gain a better understanding of both our own gender as well as our inner opposite gender.

In the next section we will take a closer look at what this means in practical day-to-day terms.

THE WORLD IS FILLED WITH MOTHERS & LITTLE BOYS

The evolution of awareness proceeds in three stages, defined as the mother, the male and the female. The purpose of evolution is not only to unfold these three aspects of awareness, but also to reconcile them in such a manner as to bring about an intelligent co-operation between them.

In the introduction to this book I made the promise that I will skirt around technical issues, and I intend to keep to that promise. Therefore those of you who would like to have more in-depth information on this section of the teachings are recommended to read my other books, in order to grasp more fully what I am merely touching upon here ever so briefly.

People don't realise it, but the world today is very much the product of that particular aspect of awareness which is characterised by what we term the mother. In fact, most of our actions, thoughts and emotions are dictated by the mother. For example: "Before you leave the house go put on some better clothing, otherwise what will people think of you?" "When you go to work today, make sure you are polite to your boss. Impolite boys are not entitled to ask for time off." "You were always told to concentrate on your schoolwork. If you had better academic qualifications you could now be earning a lot more money."

Whether this kind of dialogue is coming from your real mother, your wife, (or your husband, for that matter), your friends, or whether it is just simply in your own head, the fact remains that you still think, feel and, most important of all, behave like a small boy or girl who needs to be told what to do in order to get the approval of someone else, including, of course, the approval of mother! However, if we need to be told what to do, what to think, what to feel and what to say, how can there ever be intelligent co-operation? Every time a marriage or a romantic relationship lands on the rocks, it is without fail because the woman is in mother mode and the man is in little boy mode. In the beginning this is not too much of a problem, but once the novelty of the relationship or marriage begins to wear off, the man begins to tire of always being told what to do and the woman begins to resent the fact that she is always having to tell hubby what to do. And so the script goes something like this: (Man) "Stop telling me what to do! Do you think I'm stupid, or something?" (Woman) "Can't you think for yourself? How can you arrange to go out for drinks when you know today is my mother's birthday?" (Man) "Where are we supposed to turn off?" (Woman) "Take the next turn-off, not this one." (Man) "Why can't I take this turn-off? Who's driving this car anyway?" (Woman) "But you asked me where to turn-off!" (Man) "Yes, I know, but this turn-off is just as good as the next one!" (Man) "Would you like to go out for dinner tonight?" (Woman) "Yes, that sounds lovely." (Man) "Good! Where would you like to go?" (Woman) "Anywhere nice. You decide." (Man) "Stop being so goddamned vague! Just make up your mind, woman! I asked you where you would like to go to." (Woman) "Listen here, Pighead! If I tell you where I would like to go to, you will accuse me of always wanting to wear the blinking pants!"

Much the same kind of scenario tends to take place in the bedroom, and therefore it is also not long before the man, being eager to please mother, begins to feel very inadequate because mother is tired of being made love to by a little boy and of having to tell him what to do, and what not to do. Therefore: (Man) "Why are you so cold towards me?" (Woman) "I'm not cold. Only tired." (Man) "Well, how can I really turn you on?" (Woman) "I don't know. I've got a headache. Let's just go to sleep."

Even in the workplace this scenario also tends to play itself out in a very similar fashion, even if it is between a male boss and a male employee. This is something we will look at more closely a little later on. I am for now only trying to get across the concept that the world today is still very much controlled by the mother awareness, and by men and women trying to get the mother's approval in one way or another.

Yet, in relation to all of this, do not be fooled by the general belief that we are living in a patriarchal society. The fact that the male gods seem to have triumphed over the female goddesses of antiquity, and the fact that the world is only just beginning to emerge out of a huge swamping over of sexual inequality, male chauvinism and female suppression, is merely the result of little boys having temporarily rebelled against the tyrannical rule of the mother. But throughout all of this rebellion, mother has emerged intact, somewhat dishevelled and, needless to say, not at all pleased! The end result? Men, or rather, the little boys, have been brought sharply to their knees, and feeling awfully sheepish and guilty about their misdemeanours, are now bending over backwards to try and please mother more than ever before!

And now? Well, clearly, all the valiant knights in shining armour are gone and so too are the brave hunters of yesteryear. In a world that has to pay for its crime against mother, there is no place for heroes! In fact, the heroes had their chance, screwed up (excuse the pun), and must not again be given the chance to overrun the authority of mother.

So now what? Well, now I think that perhaps you can begin to see that it is intelligent co-operation that is needed, and not rebellion or suppression. The mother has her place, and is therefore not meant to be annihilated or suppressed. It is more a question of little boys having to grow up and, in growing up, gaining the ability to see the value in mother's wisdom, and then seeking out ways in which to co-operate with her, rather than remaining firmly attached to her apron strings. In other words, it is time for men to become true males, because no mother has a problem trusting a son who has proved his ability as a hunter. But no woman in her right mind is ever going to trust a little boy who only proves his irresponsibility time and time again, and then wants to be rude about it as well!

So then, what is a true male and, for that matter, where does the true female fit into all of this? We will shortly be looking at what is meant by the true male and female, but what we have discovered so far is that essentially the female is dual in nature, that is, every female has two sides to her; the mother and the woman.

FOUR

TERM 2:
CHANGING YOUR SELF-IMAGE

If you wish to change you must cast off your self-image.

We come now to the second demand of Captain Life, namely, "You must not bring with you any clothing or shoes of any description, but you may clothe yourself in only a white cotton sheet." Quite simply, this means that you should cast off your old self-image and clothe yourself in natural simplicity.

The biggest bugbear in people's lives is that their self-image tends to trip them up again and again. Self-image is a complex thing, and it is made up of everything you believe about yourself, including your self-esteem, or the value you place upon yourself.

People tend to look upon themselves in terms of being, for example, a married woman who has a husband, children, a career as a school teacher, a hobby, a certain temperament, a particular talent or two and, of course, a name and a family lineage. But realise that all of these accessories, for that is exactly what these amount to, are only possible to have by virtue of the fact that we have physical bodies. How could you be a mother without a body? Or how could you express your talent, say for playing a musical instrument, without physical hands to do so? Likewise, your family lineage and name are purely dependent upon you having a physical presence. And yet, are you your body? Some people think they are! Others think they are their minds. Some think they are a combination of body, mind and spirit, or soul, or something equally vague and nebulous like that. And, of course, some just don't think at all!

What do you think? Have you ever thought about it? For myself, I can only say that I honestly do not know. However, what I do know is that I am not my body, or my emotions, or my mind, for I can control all of these, and the fact that I can control what I do, feel and think, suggests that somewhere behind all of this is a being that I am only slowly getting to know. That being, I realise, is my true self — a being that astounds me again and again, for on the one hand it is so vast, so mysterious and so highly complex, that often I stand in breathless wonder at the truly magical abilities of that inner creature we call man. And yet, that inner being is also simplicity itself and because of this, it is only by adopting a childlike (as opposed to childish) simplicity that we can begin to grasp our awesome potential as human beings. In other words, it is only when we put aside all of our endless clutter, and fall quiet, very quiet, that we can begin to sense who and what we really are.

So what then of self-image? The answer is really quite simple. If you are not your body, then stop feeling so terrible about yourself because you have thighs big enough to kick-start a Boeing, or because you have a face that looks like the backend of a bus. If you are not your emotions, then stop indulging in feeling so guilty because you have a violent temper. If you are not your mind, then stop feeling so stupid because you are not a computer boffin. And in short, if you are not your status as a married woman, a mother, a school teacher and whatever else, then stop fretting that you must be an awful person because your husband is having an affair, your son is homosexual and a drug addict, your teenage daughter is pregnant and half your students at school are failing their examinations. Rather get to know yourself, and then maybe you will begin to see why all these "terrible" things are happening in your life. But in order to do that you must first put aside all of this junk you carry around for baggage, and adopt a simple approach to life.

The simplest approach we can possibly take is a childlike approach and, as with any child, first things come first, and what makes them first is the fact that they are happening right here right now! So, I take a good look at myself, and what do I see? I see that I have a physical body, (never mind what it looks like), which is distinctly different to that of another person who, for some unknown reason, is called a woman. Now! There is woman and here is me, called a man, also for some unknown reason. But what does that mean? No child is really ever too worried about technical definitions, for they are far more interested in the "doings" of the thing being scrutinised. So the natural question is, what do men and women do?

From the little we have learned so far, we do at least know that the male is the hunter. But it is important to remember also that we all have an inner counterpart. Therefore, females have an inner male, just as males have an inner female. We also know that, as the hunter, the man knows that he needs to be in harmony with the world around him if he is going to be successful in tracking game and prey, and survive. This is irrespective of whether the prey happens to be a real animal or whether it is some other "animal", say in the form of a business venture. However, we now need to look somewhat more closely at exactly what is entailed here, and the first point is that we cannot afford to go hunting with a self-image that keeps tripping us up. "Hey, you lion! Who do you think you are growling at me?" "Oh! You slimy frog! Get your nasty little butt off my foot!" "Listen here, arsehole! I sell good green beans, so don't come in here telling me my beans are old!" "I beg your pardon, but can you please not paw my beautiful garments with your rather filthy hands!" If you are going to hunt down prey, you cannot afford to have an "attitude problem". But not to have an "attitude problem" means that you must be willing to detach yourself from your self-image or, better still, get rid of it altogether.

Remember that magical word — detach. It is your only defense against the debilitating traps set by your self-image. Whenever you are facing a potential challenge, remind yourself to detach from your self-image. If you don't, you will find yourself having all your buttons pushed and you will pounce upon your prey with huge abandon and an almighty scream, stabbing passionately with your spear! Until, eventually, you come to realise that you are stabbing at thin air, that your prey has slipped away unnoticed, and that the smell of blood everywhere is the smell of your own blood. Quite simply, you have stabbed yourself in the foot. Does this sound familiar? But, of course, what is even worse, is the fact that sometimes, when eventually you do come to your senses, you realise with horror that the little furry animal you tried to spear down so passionately has turned out to be a lion who is not at all impressed with your heroic hunting! Your boss at work? In such cases it is always painfully clear to see with hindsight that it would perhaps have been wiser to be more "in tune", to be more in harmony, with the world around you!

ACHIEVING HARMONY THROUGH CONFLICT

All awareness is relative — terms such as male and female are not absolutes, but values we temporarily attach to a given state of awareness relative to any other state of awareness.

In trying to work with our self-image, the first thing we need to get into its proper perspective is that the terms "man" and "woman" denote physical gender, whereas "male" and "female" denote the particular state of awareness that is constantly being used by both genders. We term this phenomenon the relative factor of awareness.

We also need to mention that all of awareness evolves through two main mediums: one, the universal law known as Harmony through Conflict; and two, the phenomenon we term the mirror concept. As strange as this may seem, it is only through conflict that we are able to evolve new knowledge, for where there is no conflict there is also no incentive, and neither is there any momentum, to uncover something new. In order to gain new knowledge, and thereby to evolve our awareness, we need to be challenged, and any challenge invariably gives rise to some sort of conflict, even if this is merely internal conflict, like, for example, when we think one thing but feel another. The mirror concept we have already discussed, although I urge you to read up on this all-important concept in my other books.

Because of people's low self-image, the Law of Harmony through Conflict is mostly ignored. Instead of men and women welcoming the challenges in their lives, they tend to bemoan their ill-luck at having so much conflict to cope with. Yet, as we have already pointed out, without conflict the evolution of awareness would cease, and life would rapidly become empty of all meaning and purpose. To understand this is really not very difficult, provided that we look at life with total honesty, for if we do, we quickly enough come to realise that any conflict situation is merely an opportunity to practise intelligent co-operation, either with another person, or simply with the world around us. Let us look at an example.

Say you take your car to the garage to be serviced, but when you get it back you find that the work has not been carried out to your satisfaction. Clearly, you have several options open to you. Firstly, you could say and do nothing, except go home to scream at your wife about the garage's bad workmanship. Secondly, you could send your wife back to the garage the following day to fight your battle for you, under the pretext that you are too busy and therefore don't have the time. Thirdly, you could phone your lawyer and ask him to fight your battle for you, in which case it will cost you! Fourthly, you could get your own low self-image to fight your battle for you, in which case you hand your control over to that little tyrant, and let rip at the staff of the garage, shouting and screaming and performing like a real arsehole, and ending up with threatening not to pay for the work. If you go that route, you will antagonise everyone, get no-one's co-operation, and most of the time you will leave, spitting mad and not really having got anywhere at all.

As an alternative, you could look at the situation in terms of it being a challenge to gain more knowledge through the medium of your own experience, in which case it will be empowering, in the sense of knowledge or power that you have yourself gained. Should you choose to go this route, then you must always bear in mind that the power lies in the moment, and therefore you must act immediately, or at least as soon as you possibly can. By taking action, all you need to do is to go straight to the manager and state your case, politely, but firmly, and make it quite clear that you find the workmanship unacceptable. It is as simple as that, and I have yet to see negative results from such an approach. Most people, if approached with an attitude of, "Look! We have a problem here. Can we please talk about it and resolve it," will do whatever it takes to please you. On the other hand, any person approached with an attitude of, "Look, here! You have made a bugger-up of my car," will immediately give in to his or her own low self-image, dig in his or her heels and become very unco-operative, to say the least.

In all these circumstances the important point to bear in mind is that people are not there to victimise us, but are in our lives in order to provide us with opportunity to gain, or hunt for, experience, knowledge and, of course, power, irrespective of whether the challenges they provide us with are positive or negative. In reality, every one of your acts is an act of hunting, no matter whether you are hunting for service, hunting for food, (as in shopping), hunting for warmth (as in friendship), hunting for a job, a better salary or extra leave.

If you remember that you are merely on a hunting expedition, then you will also remember that others also have their own baggage, fears, doubts and, above all, low self-images. Normally, if you are out trout fishing, or shooting, you will not get all upset and feel hard-done-by and victimised if the trout avoids your hook, or if the buck you encounter are so inconsiderate as to bolt the moment they set eyes on you. In this respect people are no different, for the simple reason that they know you are hunting them, just like they too are hunting someone or something else. So, if you want the buck to stand still so that you can shoot it, you are going to have to stalk it with care, and not just run up to it shouting that you cannot survive without food. Likewise, if you want your boss to grant you an increase in salary, then you are also going to have to stalk him with care, and not simply blunder into his office telling him that you cannot survive on such a low salary!

But what does it mean to stalk? Stalking is quite simply a type of manipulation that is carried out with the express purpose of getting the other person to do what you want him or her to do, *but so that you will both benefit from that act*. Ordinarily, plain manipulation means forcing another person into doing your bidding for your own self-centred gain, but at the other person's expense. However, stalking means getting the other person to co-operate with you intelligently, so that both of you can benefit and therefore win. The usual practice of manipulation is very much to do with playing the blame game, for it is always you and the world out there, and the world is never doing what it is you want it to do. But stalking has its basis, not in blame, but in inclusivity, and the approach of inclusivity is, "Everything that is happening right now is an opportunity for both myself and my opponent to gain in knowledge and in power." To see how this works, let us return to the example of having had a bad car service.

So, you go to the manager of the garage, and you politely but firmly inform him that you are not satisfied with the service, and you tell him why you are not satisfied. Already you have manipulated this man, Rudi, not only into giving you his full attention, but also into taking action on your behalf. What's more, by not blaming Rudi, you are manipulating him out of becoming defensive, and into seeking co-operation with you to find a solution to the problem, which, of course, is not really a problem at all, but an opportunity for both of you to gain new knowledge through experience. Whatever happens after this point will depend very much on how carefully and skillfully you stalk Rudi! You can ask to be transported back to your office, or your home, whilst the problem is being sorted out, or you could get Rudi to give you a courtesy car to use in the meantime. But one way or the other, if you concentrate on getting Rudi to co-operate with you, you will get your car properly serviced at no extra cost or any real inconvenience to yourself. In addition, both you and Rudi will come away from this experience having gained a lot more knowledge than either of you had before, because otherwise there would have been no point in having the experience in the first place.

Although at this point you may have hundreds of questions about stalking, you only need to start trying to practise stalking to see that it is not really all that difficult. Any situation, irrespective of whether you are stalking your boss, your husband or your kids, always brings the principle of intelligent co-operation into being. Therefore, if you feel as if you are being victimised, then take it as fact that you are not stalking anybody, but instead, playing the blame game. And because you are playing the blame game, your mirrors must reflect for you your own sense of blame. By trying to blame someone else for your challenge, you can be sure that either that same person, or another, will in turn blame you for something else, in which case, you will of course once again be the victim!

If you can remember here to approach life from the angle of seeking intelligent co-operation, you can never really lose, because if you seek co-operation you will get co-operation, and once you have that co-operation you can utilise even apparent "failures" to gain knowledge, and therefore power. However, in order to achieve intelligent co-operation, as opposed to just a reluctant or even a resentful co-operation, which never yields a satisfactory result, you must always bear in mind the relative factor of awareness which we will now look at in greater detail.

WHILST MAN & WOMAN RELATE TO GENDER, THE TERMS MALE & FEMALE RELATE TO SPECIFIC STATES OF AWARENESS

Intelligence gives rise to awareness, but all awareness has two polarities, one termed male because it is masculine in quality, and the other, being feminine in quality, termed female.

We are so caught up in our social conditioning that we simply assume that being a man means that we must always be masculine, and that being a woman means that we must always be feminine. As a result, our self-images suffer terribly when we discover that our circumstances in life often demand that we play a role which is the opposite of our gender. For example, if you are a man working for a boss who is also a man, you will often feel emasculated because, in your eyes, he is not respecting you as a man. Worse still, if as a man you work for a female boss, you will more than likely feel extremely emasculated as a result of having to take orders from a woman. However, in both situations this is just a fact of life, and it has absolutely nothing to do with being less of a man because you are taking your orders from another man or from a woman.

All of life is relative. Since life revolves around awareness, and since awareness itself has two polarities, namely, male and female, life must always be relative to the awareness experienced in the moment. Therefore, in working for a man, you will be female relative to your boss, irrespective of your gender, and in working for a woman, you will still be female, no matter how good a male you may be. Likewise, if you go shopping, then you, as the client, are masculine relative to the shop owner, even if he is a man and you are a woman. The weekly maid who comes to work in your home, too, is female relative to you the housewife. And your children, irrespective of their genders, will all be female relative to you as the mother.

It is not really possible in this book to explain all the technical issues involved here, so let us simply say that whenever you take orders from someone you are in female mode, and whenever you give the orders you are in male mode. We say that the male gives the direction because he has a purpose to fulfil, whilst the female takes the male's lead in order to fulfil his purpose, and this invariably allows her to fulfil her purpose.

This should not be taken as implying that men are better than women, but simply that men and women are equal but different. In other words, men and women are equally important but they have different functions, and therefore have different roles to play in life. These functions and roles are derived entirely from the two polarities of awareness: male and female. We didn't invent these two polarities, but we have discovered how to work with them, in order to achieve harmony and co-existence.

Say you are a man and you need an income. You decide to go and work for someone who has a business, and therefore a purpose. If you want that job and if you wish to keep it, then you had better take your orders from that man and fulfil his purpose. Only in that way can you fulfil your own purpose, which is to have an income. If, on the other hand, you don't like taking orders from anyone, then stop complaining about having to take orders and become your own boss, in which case you can then give the orders. Likewise, if you are a woman and want a husband, rather than a little boy, then give him the pants to wear. If you don't, you may well have a marriage, but I can assure you that you will not have a husband in the true sense of the word. Instead you will be in mother mode and having a relationship with a little boy! If that is what you want, then by all means be a mother, but stop complaining about the fact that your husband is having an affair with the pretty little secretary at his office who is always so eager to take his lead.

Because of the two polarities, working with the different roles is bound to bring out conflict in one way or another, even if this is only in the sense of feeling threatened by masculinity or femininity. For example, how often as a woman do you not feel inferior to men? Or, as a man, how often do you not feel inadequate in the presence of women?

But, as we have already noted, the purpose of conflict is to bring forth new knowledge, and so, if you are going to achieve intelligent co-operation with the world around you, then you must start to take careful note of the roles that you play in life. Therefore, when, irrespective of gender, are you required to give the male lead, and when are you required to take the male's lead?

This then brings us straight back to the concept of intelligent co-operation, rather than begrudging co-operation, or behaving like a bull in a china shop. Life, and what you get out of life, is entirely dependent upon whether you co-operate with the world around you begrudgingly, or intelligently, or whether you behave like an insane bull. And all of this depends upon your self-image, how well you understand yourself, and how and what you feel about yourself as a result of that understanding. However, in order to get a better grasp on all of this, we must return to the concept of hunting, for clearly, it is very much a matter of hunting for understanding that we are considering here.

THE ROLE OF THE HUNTER

*The hunter, irrespective of gender,
is masculine.*

People often have really strange ideas about why their relationships do not work, and this is primarily because they seem to believe that as long as they have a man's body, or a woman's body, then they are quite automatically male or female respectively. Although this should in theory be so, from what we have seen so far, it should be starting to become clear that in practice the male and female energies are factors of awareness and that they are relative to one another. Therefore, if your gender is masculine, then irrespective of the fact that your chest might resemble a woolly carpet, or that you may be better endowed than a horse, you still have to learn to materialise your masculine potential and thereby discover what it is to be truly male. Likewise, if your gender is feminine, then even if you wear the most exotically feminine perfume, paint your lips a bright red and have breasts that make the assets of Dolly Parton look like poached eggs in comparison, you will still drive every true male away from you if you insist upon telling him what to do, how to do it and when to do it, for, in spite of your attributes you have done nothing to materialise your true potential as a female.

To see this in action, take the example of you and

your best friend deciding to go fishing. Your friend suggests that you go to a certain river, but although you know fishing is poor in that spot, you agree anyway. In such a case, no matter how hairy your chest is, you are female relative to your friend, because you are simply taking his lead. Likewise, if you invite your girlfriend out to dinner, but insist that she decides where you go, what wine to drink and what food to eat, then once again you will be female relative to her, for irrespective of your horselike endowments, you are still behaving like a little boy on an outing with his mother.

Clearly, if you are a man and you want to make use of your masculine potential by trying to be a true male, then even if you want to be polite to both your friend and your girlfriend, you must still provide the lead where necessary. In this way, if your friend suggests a poor fishing spot, you will take the male lead by pointing out that fishing in that spot is poor, but at the same time you will also offer a few other suggestions. In this case you will be acting like a true male, in that you will be providing the lead, but you will also not be emasculating your friend, for although you are giving the lead, you are still allowing him to co-operate intelligently with you in deciding to which other spot you will be going. In other words, by not simply taking his lead, and yet also by allowing him to take the lead in deciding which of the alternatives you suggested is going to be your destination, you make it possible for both of you to be male and you avoid bulldozing your friend into taking your lead.

Exactly the same is true of your girlfriend. By taking the lead in deciding which restaurant you should go to, you can still be polite by telling her beforehand where you intend going, and by asking her if she has an aversion to that particular place. If by any chance she does indeed dislike the place, then you could suggest another restaurant. The same goes for the wine you order, but in all these cases you will be the true male because you are giving the lead and, at the same time, intelligently initiating her co-operation, rather than negating her wishes or her feelings.

From the angle of the woman, exactly the same principles apply. For example, if you wish to be courted by a particular man, then you must stalk him into doing so. In other words, you must hunt, not only him, but also the relationship. However, if you go about this in a masculine way, and if he is a true male, (otherwise why on earth would you want a relationship with him?), he will take one look at you and run a mile. If you want to hunt such a man, and hunt him you will have to, then you must hunt him by taking the lead in the sense of being as female as you possibly can. By being a true female, by seeking intelligent co-operation with him and by making it clear that you wish to take his lead, you will evoke in that man every bit of masculinity he has, and in no time at all the poor fellow will be so male that he will even ask you to marry him. Yet, realise that in having taken the lead in being female, you have in effect been as male as male can be, and not only that, but in hunting him, you have also been male. In other words, by being a true female, you have used your own inner male to do your hunting for you! This is true, even in the workplace, for if you are a female boss, and you want your male employees to excel at their duties, then you should strive to evoke in them their masculine potential as true males, even though, relative to them, you are still very much male by virtue of being their boss.

Similarly, if a man wants to court you, he will allow his own inner female to tie you up into all sorts of little bows. By being utterly charming and open, he will not only hang onto your every word, but he will also be quite passionate in seeking your intelligent co-operation. Listening attentively to every word you say and to every wish you express, such a man will be deeply sensitive and, following his intuition, he will use his feelings to guide him into being the best male you have ever known. Yet, although such a man is being a true male in hunting you, he is nonetheless using his inner female to feel how best to evoke the female in you.

The important point to remember is that, regardless of your gender, it is the male who is the hunter. But also bear in mind that, in order to be able to track game successfully, the hunter must be clever enough to outwit his prey.

However, to outwit one's prey implies stalking and, at the end of the day, any stalking manoeuvre is nothing other than intelligent co-operation, for, as we saw in the examples above, both men and women need to co-operate intelligently with their own inner counterparts in order to get the willing co-operation of the world around them. All of life is simply the product of intelligent co-operation firstly, between ourselves and our own inner counterparts; and secondly, between our masculine or feminine potential and the world around us.

So, if life is "good", it is because you are good at achieving intelligent co-operation. But if life is "bad", then this is because you lack the necessary skill in achieving that intelligent co-operation. If your life is not working, what this means is that, irrespective of your gender, it is the male in you that is not good at hunting. What does this really amount to?

THE RULES OF INTELLIGENT CO-OPERATION

*The quintessence of masculinity is harmony, just as the
quintessence of hunting is intelligent co-operation.*

We have already seen that as the hunter the male knows the importance of having to be in harmony with the world around him. Living in harmony with the world around us is really a combination of several concepts that are all completely interrelated and interdependent. Let's look at what this means in practical terms.

First of all, in order to be able to track and to trap prey, the hunter must be intimately familiar with his world and yet remain detached from it. If you, for example, wish to make a business venture successful, then you must become one hundred percent familiar with the nature of your trade. Not to know all the ins and outs of that trade is to invite failure. Likewise, if your child is a drug addict and you want to help him, then it is vital for you to familiarise yourself fully with every facet of that problem — why the child chose the drug experience in the first place; what the drug is, and what both the short and the long term effects of using it are; what the relationship of that child is in relation to you as the parent, in relation to his peers and to the world in general. In short, unless you are so familiar with your child's drug problem that it could well be your own, you will never be able to help him, for merely to tell him to be a good boy and not do it again is not going to help!

However, being fully familiar with one's world creates its own lethal trap. A hunter can become so familiar with the animals he is stalking that, in time, he finds himself incapable of hunting them. Quite simply, the hunter has grown to love the animals so much that he cannot bring himself to kill them, much less eat them! How many times does it not happen that a man becomes so engrossed in his business that it becomes his everything at the cost of all else, including his family and his health? Similarly, how often do parents of drug addicts not take the required action because they love their children too much to be ruthless? And how often do partners in a romantic relationship not speak up because they are afraid they will hurt the other one's feelings? In all such cases the hunter has become so involved with his prey, whether this is his business, his problem child or his spouse, that his judgement has become impaired. Refusing to see the challenge for what it truly is, such a man or woman loses all objectivity, and instead of being the hunter, has become the hunted.

This is the reason why it is so very important to stand detached at all times. Being detached does not mean that you do not care — on the contrary, it means you care so deeply that you do not hesitate to be as ruthless as you need to be in order to fulfil your mission. If you are in business, but refuse to be ruthlessly competitive, you will fail. Likewise, if you are having to handle a child who is addicted to drugs, but if you refuse to take a ruthless approach, the drugs will win every time and your child will be destroyed. What then do you want? Do you love your business so much that you allow it to destroy your family and yourself? Do you love your fellow businessmen so much that you allow them to destroy you? Do you love your child so much that you allow the drugs to destroy him or her? What kind of love is that?

Real love is born of ruthlessness, which starts with detachment — a detachment that enables the hunter to hunt his prey successfully. The hunter is able to be ruthless and detached because he knows himself so well, and he knows for a fact that he does not plunder his world. This leads us to the second of the concepts.

The hunter cares very deeply for the world around him and, as a result, also respects it. Because of that caring and that respect, the hunter never plunders his world, but takes from it only what he truly needs. Never does the true hunter take just for the sake of taking, and never does he hunt just for the fun of it. If the truth be told, the true hunter never does like hunting, he just does it incredibly well. That's all! Although there are plenty of people in this world who have to face the challenge of child abuse, no true parent takes a delight in punishing his or her child.

Likewise, although there are more than enough people in this world who have to learn the lessons of inflicting pain, the true surgeon does not cut open his patients upon an insane whim.

Think deeply about this for as long as you need to, in order to grasp the importance of what I am saying here. However, one final word of caution — do not take the world at face value. For example, consider a boss who sees the potential in a young employee who is loyal and hardworking. By offering him increases, promotions, etc., he will get that employee to work even harder, give even more of his time, his devotion and his enthusiasm, until finally the employee has become nothing more than a money-making machine for his boss. Having given up everything else in his life for the sake of his career, such an employee will go from being an enthusiastic free-thinking young man, into a miserable wretch who has traded all for greed and success. Yet the real culprit is his boss, who has not only enticed him, but also exploited his natural drive and enthusiasm. But by far the worst thing about all this is the fact that such an employee will normally be hugely grateful to his boss for having made all of this possible. How caring is such a boss? Similarly, how loving is any parent who manipulates his or her child into following a career that the child hates, and all in the name of what is good for the child?

The third concept is really an extension of the first, namely, that the hunter knows the routines of the game he is hunting. What this amounts to is that the hunter has to be something of a psychologist and understand through experience that the routine acts and predictable behaviour of both man and animal are the only traps he ever needs to set. It is only the inexperienced hunter who needs to set traps, because once you know the routines of, say, a rabbit, you simply need to lie in wait for it, and when it comes hopping round its favourite bush at its favourite time of the day, you simply pick it up by the ears! I am, of course, speaking about human rabbits. Animal rabbits have very good noses, and therefore are not quite so stupid and unsuspecting as humans tend to be!

That is the reason why it is so very important to study the game one is intending to hunt. For example, if you wish to have a better relationship with your boss at work, then you should get to know and understand his behaviour patterns for what they mean to him. As you do so you will quickly enough note what affects his moods, how certain mood swings can affect his thinking, as well as his actions, and how best to bring about in him a change of mood. Therefore, if you need to ask him for a raise in salary, you will be wise not to do something which you know will put him into a foul mood, but you should instead do everything that you know will make him feel secure, contented, happy and open-handed. In other words, by knowing the routine actions, emotions and thought patterns of a person, you can always use that knowledge to your advantage. This is after all what is meant by stalking!

Which brings us straight to the fourth concept. By knowing the routines of his prey, the hunter is clever enough to outwit his prey. Although this sounds so much like common sense, it is truly amazing how often people will abandon good old-fashioned common sense in favour of some truly harebrained scheme or plot! It's obvious that if a hunter were to set his traps in such a way that they were conspicuous, no animal would be crazy enough to walk into them, least of all that animal called your boss, your wayward spouse or your delinquent child. For this reason, the really good hunter will not necessarily reveal his real motive until the trap is sprung. Just think of stalking your boss into giving you a salary raise, or think about confronting your spouse about having an illicit affair, and you will see soon enough how this works.

And now, the final concept, and a very important one at that, is that the hunter is clever enough to know that just as he is a hunter hunting someone or something, so is everyone else also a hunter hunting him! Therefore, when your son suddenly tidies up his room, does all his schoolwork and the dishes without you having to goad him into doing it, then take it as fact he is stalking you for something. Likewise, when your boss suddenly comes to you with a bunch of roses, gives you an increase in salary, and gives you the afternoon off on top of it, don't become ecstatic. Instead become outwardly ecstatic, as you are expected to do, (this is only good stalking), but become inwardly hyper-alert. Above all, and no matter what your personal opinion of your boss may be, remember that he would not be your boss if his skills at stalking were not better than yours.

Clearly, if it is so easy for you to learn to pick up a rabbit by its ears because of its predictable routines, then as a hunter you would be extremely careless to be predictable yourself. A hunter will only ever behave in a predictable manner if he wants to be picked up — a very good ploy to use on someone who is already an accomplished hunter and therefore very unpredictable in his or her own routines. Consequently, if you don't want to be the next rabbit, then your own movements and actions must become unpredictable. For example, if your marriage is rocky, and you suspect that your husband may be having an affair with someone else, then it is just plain stupid always to go and play bridge on Thursday evenings from 18h00 to 23h00. If you do, you will just be inviting trouble. If, on the other hand, you vary your routines, there is much less chance of him having an affair, and the likelihood is that by having become unpredictable you will have eliminated the boredom in your marriage, which might well also turn out to be the cause of your problems. In any event, bear in mind that predictability means that you are not being fluid, and in not being fluid you will invariably be stubborn, forceful and domineering, opinionated and, above all, just plain boring! Who wants to remain faithful to such a jerk?

USING CONFLICT TO UNCOVER NEW KNOWLEDGE

Only through conflict can new knowledge come into being.

People fear conflict instead of welcoming it. This does not mean that you must go around picking a fight with all and sundry, but it does mean that when conflict does arise of its own accord, then you should not run away from it, but face it, own it and use it to your advantage. To put this in a nutshell, "If your picture doesn't match my picture, then it means that somewhere we are both missing a connecting link", and that missing link is without fail new knowledge.

It is just plain stupid to keep on insisting that if your picture does not match my picture then one of us has to be wrong. Who says? Why can't we both be right? Or are you going to insist that if I am right then you must be "righter"?

Only by understanding this fact can conflict be used constructively by the true hunter, and provided that this is grasped by even just one of the people concerned, new knowledge will be uncovered. Remember that the person who understands this fact will not be working towards fuelling the conflict, but will instead be working towards using the conflict which is already there in order to uncover the new knowledge. But what is even more important, is the fact that by utilising the conflict to bring forth new knowledge, the hunter is in effect transmuting something which is negative into something that is positive, and herein lies the deeper meaning of achieving harmony through conflict.

The million dollar question here, is, "How do I achieve this?" The answer is quite simple, and we have already been discussing it, namely, intelligent co-operation. If you are now feeling perplexed and at a loss, you have been reading too fast and not paying proper attention. Therefore go back and reread the bit on intelligent co-operation, and you are bound to find the lights coming on!

We have already seen that all of awareness is relative and, as a result, men are not always in male mode and neither are women always in female mode. Let's look at this a little deeper. Consider a mother and her young son.

In guiding her children, a mother has no option other than to draw from her own experience in life which, of course, is her knowledge. This means that the mother measures her children's behaviour against what she knows to be good behaviour, that is, behaviour which is beneficial not only to the child, but also to the world around it. But realise that by acting in this way, the mother is working with the known which, as we know, is the function of the male.

The son, on the other hand, not yet having sufficient experience of life upon the physical plane, is facing the unknown, and therefore he automatically listens to his mother's guidance. Because he is taking her lead, he is female relative to his mother. This does not mean that such a boy thinks of himself as being a little girl. On the contrary, if he is really listening to his mother, he will even be learning from her how a man is supposed to function in the world. But the bottom line is still that any child, irrespective of gender, does not have the required experience of life, and therefore has to listen to its mother, whether he or she likes it or not. Only by listening to the mother, and then either by following her guidance, or by ignoring her guidance, does the boy begin to gather his own knowledge through experience. But either way, the child is female relative to his mother, for it does not matter whether he takes his mother's guidance in the sense of doing what he has been told, or whether he takes that guidance in the sense of finding out what is the result if he doesn't conform to it, the fact remains that he is taking her guidance in one form or another.

Exactly the same is true amongst adults, especially in the workplace. Think of a man working for a male employer. Such an employee mostly never really knows enough about the company he is working for to take the male lead, and neither is he required to do so. The only thing that should be clear to an employee, is the job description. In other words, he knows what his duties and his function in the company are, for these have been spelled out to him when he took on the job. But in fulfilling the requirements of his job description, he is automatically female relative to his employer, even though he may be the best male in the whole world.

This is a point that can never be stressed enough, for the simple reason that all too often, because of social conditioning, men feel emasculated as a result of not being able to take the male lead in their working environment. Yet, this is so unnecessary, if only such men would understand that in spite of the fact that they will always be female relative to their employers, they can still be very much male by seeking and initiating intelligent co-operation, rather than moping around waiting to be given orders. In fact very few employers want male employees that are forever sulking because they have to take orders. Most employers welcome men who are masculine enough to think for themselves and take the initiative, provided of course that such an employee does not go into direct competition with the employer.

The real male knows for a fact that he is a good male, and because of this, does not feel threatened by having to take orders from a superior. It is always those men who for some reason or other doubt their own masculinity, that tend to be highly aggressive and defensive, and who also quickly feel insulted and emasculated when told what to do.

Exactly the same is true of women. The women who

know the true meaning of being female never have a problem with taking the male lead. But those women who feel inferior, and therefore threatened by males in some way, will forever kick against taking the male lead, and will instead try to outdo the males in every possible way. You know that old song from "Annie Get Your Gun" - *Anything You Can Do I Can Do Better?* The end result of this is what I term a second-rate male, for although such a woman will be able to run a business, drive a truck and mow a lawn better than most men, she is still a woman who is not living up to her true potential, which is feminine, and therefore she can at best be second-rate.

But it is not only women who can become second-rate males, for if you look around, you will also see plenty of men who have become second-rate females. "Yes, dear. Anything you say, dear." "Yes, boss. Can I give your dog my breakfast, Sir." "Yes, pretty little Ms. Secretary. I'm very flattered that you should want a relationship with me. Do you want me to have you on the desk, or shall I rent a room in a hotel?" Such men are not providing the male lead, and in not living up to their masculine potential, they make very poor substitutes for the genuine female, who is by no means anybody's doormat. But then, if you don't believe in your own masculinity, it is also easy to associate your beard and hairy chest with a doormat!

So, what then is the bottom line in everything we have

been looking at? The answer: intelligent co-operation, of course. Intelligent co-operation with who, with what? Ah! Now you ask the real million dollar question, and the answer is: before you can begin to co-operate with anything or anybody, let alone intelligently, you first need to come to grips with your own potential, for realise that it is very difficult to co-operate intelligently when you don't even know who and what you are. Consequently, if you are a second-rate male or a second-rate female, your idea of being intelligent will be how best to outdo the opposite sex, and your idea of co-operation will be how best to walk all over the opposite sex. True intelligent co-operation can only be achieved firstly, when you know what it is to be true to your gender; secondly, when you understand that in order to get to know your own potential, regardless of whether it is masculine or feminine, you need experience, that is, knowledge; and thirdly, that knowledge can only arise through conflict of sorts. For example, how often in this book have I not pushed your buttons? You see! Conflict! Yet if you are still reading, then you are well on your way to practising intelligent co-operation and uncovering new knowledge. Remember what I explained at the beginning — intelligent co-operation means just that — co-operate intelligently! But to be intelligent about something does not mean you have to like it.

To understand how this operates in practice let us review our previous examples. In the example of the mother and her son, what can we see? As we all know from experience, the son will have one way of looking at things, and his mother another. So the end result is conflict. But this conflict is good, in the sense that it is necessary. Therefore the boy is not a bad child, he is only trying to gain his own knowledge. Are you bad because you are reading this book? It just shows you how insane social conditioning can be! No! The boy can only possibly be a bad boy if he does not co-operate intelligently with his mother in trying to uncover his own knowledge through experience. But then, for that matter, so too will the mother be a bad mother if she refuses to co-operate intelligently with her son, if she sees him as a bad boy because he is not listening to her every word, and if she denies him the opportunity to acquire his own knowledge through experience.

In the example of employee and employer, the employee is not bad when he speaks up to his employer for what he believes in. He will only be bad when he is not living up to his masculine potential and thereby not practising intelligent co-operation with his employer. In such a case, the employee will do one of two things. Either he will behave like a doormat who simply carries out every order given to him without question or, because he feels threatened by his employer, he will constantly be trying to make his employer wrong, in which case he is again not practising intelligent co-operation.

Likewise with the employer. The employer will not be less of a male if he practises intelligent co-operation with his male employees by taking into account their experiences of what is taking place in the business. If, on the other hand, he flatly refuses to listen to his male employees, he will not be practising intelligent co-operation, and mainly because he himself feels threatened by other males.

Realise that there will always be conflict of sorts, even if it is only at the level of "I don't see it your way." But every time this happens, it is always, but always, intelligent co-operation that is called for, because only in this way can new knowledge be brought forth. This knowledge is the only thing which is important — whether it is the knowledge a boy needs in order to know what it means to be a true male; whether it is the knowledge both employee and employer need in order to have a good working relationship; or whether it is the knowledge that is needed for a business to succeed. Conflict cannot be avoided, for it is necessary in order to learn how to practise intelligent co-operation, and it is only through practising intelligent co-operation that new knowledge can be acquired.

In co-operating with the opposite sex, the same principles come into play. Men are not the same as women, and their roles are not the same either. Therefore forget about trying to turn your wife into a second-rate version of yourself, and stop trying to turn your husband into a second-rate version of what you think women are all about. Just start from the point that as man and woman you are equal but different, in that your respective potentials are equal but opposite. If you remember that, then you will not expect each other to see things your way, but you will instead strive to see each other's point of view. By doing this you will both gain a far greater perspective than each of you had before, and soon you will begin to discover that intelligent co-operation, quite apart from being fun, is also truly intelligent!

For example, let's assume that a woman, Anna, says to her husband, Stan, "I don't know why I am saying this, but I feel that there is something wrong with our relationship." Normally what happens here is that the husband, feeling somehow accused, will quite angrily demand that his wife should explain herself. Yet, the fact is that she has already said she doesn't actually know what it is, and that it is just a feeling.

If Stan is a true male, he will not press Anna to explain to him what she is sensing. Instead he will compare what she is saying against his own database, which is what he already knows about his relationship with Anna, and which therefore constitutes what is for him part of the known. If, having done this, Stan can still not grasp what Anna is sensing, he will then try to get a feeling for what she is saying by questioning her, not in the sense of "Please explain yourself", but in the sense of "Try to tell me more." In other words, by being the male, and by initiating the act of intelligent co-operation, Stan is using his own inner female to guide both himself and Anna towards a better understanding of what it is she is sensing.

Taking Stan's lead in this respect, Anna will be using her inner male to try and make as much logical sense out of what she as a female has picked up from within the unknown. The end result of such intelligent co-operation between Stan and Anna, as well as between themselves and their own inner counterparts, is that when finally Stan does achieve a real feeling for what Anna is sensing, he will either be able to pinpoint exactly what is bothering his wife, or, by embarking upon a different line of questioning such as "Do you mean this?" or "Do you feel that?" it will not be long before Anna will be able to say, "That's it! That's exactly what I mean!"

From this example it should be becoming clear that in order to be a true male, it is vitally important for the man to learn to listen to his feelings which, in the final analysis, represent his own inner female. Likewise, for a woman to be a true female, she must also learn to listen to her feelings, but she must in addition allow her inner male to guide her towards making sense of what it is she is intuiting.

Do not ever forget that, although it is the male who is the hunter, and who has to make things work practically upon the physical plane, the male must also listen to his heart, that is, his feelings, in order to sense where best to hunt or plant his crops and when the best time for doing so will be. Until he has learned through practical experience, he has no other knowledge to work from, except his feelings. But once he has some knowledge, he will immediately start to build upon that knowledge by thinking about it rationally. Therefore, by comparing what he does not know with what he does know, he will always come up with a solution to the problem at hand.

This is equally true of the female, for since it is her task to tend to the hearth and the children, she simply has to search her inner unknown — her feelings — for the guidance she needs. Furthermore, in tending to the hearth and the children whilst her husband is out hunting, she has no option other than to turn those feelings about what she needs to do into action upon the physical plane, and because of this the female learns to think rationally. However, the difference between the two lies in the fact that because the female takes the male's lead, the woman will always search the unknown in the sense that she will try to feel what will best fulfil the purpose of the male. Therefore, if she is alone at home and she needs to act, she will invariably look at the situation in terms of "What would my husband do?" or alternatively, "If I do this, will it suit my husband?" This in no way means that the female is subservient to her husband, it simply means that she senses, or feels, that only by fulfilling his purpose can she fulfil her own purpose. Consequently, the true female will always prefer, if at all possible, to take her problems to her husband and let him come up with a solution.

Looking at how men and women operate, we can see that both first need to listen to their feelings, and then think about how best to materialise those feelings into action or solutions to a challenge. Ironically, the true male will first listen to his heart, to his feelings, and it is only after he has gained that irrational perspective that he will compare it with his rational database in order to come up with a solution. In other words, the true male first feels, then thinks. The true female, on the other hand, will first think and then feel, in the sense of having taken the male's lead, she first compares her problem with what she knows to be the male's purpose, and then she endeavours to feel what she needs to do.

However, under the impact of social conditioning, men have been taught "Think, my boy! Think!" The sad end of this tale is that men are now too frightened to do something so silly as to feel, and instead they try desperately to be as rational as possible. Therefore when a man's wife tells him that she feels something is wrong with their relationship, he thinks frantically about it, but when he cannot find a rational reason why his wife should feel that anything is wrong, angrily demands that she should explain herself, rationally, of course! Women, on the other hand, as a result of being made to feel stupid for not being logical, also desperately try to please by becoming ever more rational, until finally they have become so logical that they too are out of touch with what they are really feeling.

FIVE

TERM 3:
YOUR SHORTCOMINGS ARE YOUR TICKET TO FREEDOM

Practising intelligent co-operation implies being defenceless.

We come now to the third of Captain Life's conditions, namely, "You may wear no jewellery or weapons upon your person; only a laurel crown and a garland of wild flowers." What this means is that you must strive to feel good enough about yourself, that you do not need to impress others with your outer appearance, and neither should you be forever on the defensive. If you are truly feeling good about yourself, in the sense that you do believe you have value as a person, not in a conceited way, but in the sense of knowing from experience that you are a good male, or a good female, then you will be happy to show the rest of the world your true self. Being perfectly at peace with the way in which nature put you together, inwardly and outwardly, you will have about you an air of quiet confidence that is just as powerful as wearing a crown. Yet, that "crown" will be your own specialness, your uniqueness as an individual unit of that greater whole we term humanity.

The problem is, however, that very few people feel good about themselves, and therefore most of us are not happy to show our true self. This is because we find it almost impossible to live with our shortcomings, most especially those shortcomings which are somehow looked upon as forming part of our character. As a result very few of us ever like to own our shortcomings, and so we desperately try to hide them, even from ourselves. But the truth is that our shortcomings are nothing more than our undeveloped potential and, as such, are very much our passage to power and our ticket to freedom. Therefore not to own our shortcomings is to deny ourselves part of our potential, and if we do that, is it surprising that we end up being powerless and unhappy?

How does this work? Take the shortcoming of being stubborn. Stubbornness is really undeveloped tenacity and perseverance, which are most precious and valuable assets to have. The difference between them lies in how we use these assets. For example, if you happen to feel inferior to others, and you therefore use this asset to try to prove yourself always right, even if deep down inside you know that you are just being pigheaded, then this is not an asset, but a very real shortcoming which will do nothing for your relationships. If, on the other hand, you say to yourself, "I don't want to come across as a bigot, but I am going to persevere in overcoming my feelings of inferiority", then you are truly using your stubbornness positively, and therefore to your advantage. By tenaciously holding onto the belief that you do have value, and that you are not inferior to others, you will in time begin to see and prove this to yourself, simply because you are not prepared to just throw in the towel and give up on yourself!

Let us also look at the example of feeling inferior. For as long as you continue to believe that you are inferior, you will never be able to turn your stubbornness into tenacity and so it will always work against you, for what you are doing is using your stubbornness to hold onto the belief that you are inferior. By doing this, you will indeed prove to yourself that you are no good. If, however, you begin to look at why you feel inferior, you will soon begin to see that what makes you feel inferior is the fact that you are not so self-important and arrogant as others. In actual fact, the feeling of inferiority is only the negative expression of humility, a most honourable trait.

Therefore, instead of always feeling inferior, look at the positive side of this, and try to see humility for what it really is. If you can do this you will begin to understand that true humility is in fact unconditional love. Where there is humility there is never any sense of blame, for one can always see one's own responsibility for what is taking place in one's life. To be able to see and to own that responsibility is empowering, because we can always go on to change what we are doing if life is not what we would like it to be. Therefore instead of being a doormat, being at everybody's mercy, being a victim of circumstance, and consequently feeling hard-done-by and inferior, you can start taking action to change what you don't like, by changing yourself, your approach to life and, above all, by changing your belief in yourself.

Rather than playing the blame game, like everyone else, you will have found the necessary humility to take responsibility for your own actions. Furthermore, far from being a doormat, you will be setting the example of someone who believes enough in him, or herself to get on with their life, in the sense of "If you don't like yourself, then change yourself, instead of blaming everyone else for making you feel inferior and somehow less."

If you are not at peace with who and what you are, because you feel insecure and therefore inadequate in some way, you will be plagued constantly by fear, doubt and suspicion. As a result, not only will you be a nervous wreck, but so too will those around you, for our mirrors can never lie to us. In addition, your insecurities will rub off on them too. Above all, these insecurities will ensure that you will be quick to become defensive and, once again, because our mirrors cannot lie, those around you will also be quick to jump onto their high horses. If you wish to get others to cooperate with you intelligently, then you must acknowledge the fact that what you see in the mirror is only your own reflection!

WORKING CONSCIOUSLY WITH MIRRORS

There are no victims in this world.
Through their actions
People merely reflect for us
Our highest hopes and deepest fears.

In trying to work consciously with the concept of mirrors, the very first thing to acknowledge is that it is always a lot easier to see something in someone else than in ourselves. For example, when a friend comes to you for advice about how to cope with a particular problem, it is always very easy for you to see almost immediately what your friend should do. However, when you have exactly the same problem yourself, you suddenly find that you are at a loss as to what to do. The reason for this is that we are all too close to ourselves to be really objective, and without that objectivity things always seem to be in a muddle and therefore unclear. There are just too many personal interests, involvements, wishes, expectations, dreams, hopes, disappointments and whatever else in the way! In fact, the list can be endless. So the end of the story is that we need objectivity, and in exactly the same way as you need a mirror in which to see your face, so we also need mirrors in which to see our behaviour.

From this it is easy to see that there is no point in playing the blame game, for it stands to reason that it is just stupid to be angry with the mirror because it shows you your own ugly face! Therefore, instead of becoming all hot under the collar and therefore defensive, we need to look deeply into that mirror in order to try and understand our own behaviour. This is what we referred to earlier as, "being aware of another person's state of being". So we ask, "What in him is causing him to do such a thing?" "What in her is causing her to say that?" In other words, if your life is not working for you, (which, remember, is why you are reading this book), then have a good look at everyone around you in order to find out what emotions, feelings, thoughts, fears, doubts, insecurities, behaviour, or whatever else in *you* is giving rise to what it is that *you* are doing wrong!

When you start to look around you, the first question you should ask yourself is, "What exactly do they want from out of life?" Or, more precisely, "What exactly do I want out of life?" If you ask that question you will quickly enough come to realise that no-one is actually very sure about what they are wanting out of life. It is truly amazing to see how little people really do understand themselves and their own wishes. Take, for example, the wish, "I would like to meet someone I can marry, and who will make me happy." What for God's sake is that for a wish? How can you go through life saying, "Make me happy?" Yet that is exactly what people do, and then when the poor wretch who has been unfortunate enough to be your chosen one fails to make you happy, you attack him or her from a dizzy height for being a failure!

Clearly, if you want to be happy, then it is up to you to make yourself happy. And if you cannot make yourself happy, then who in hell's name gives you the right to demand that someone else should make you happy? So the second point we need to consider is the fact that whatever you do for yourself, or to yourself, automatically affects all those around you. Therefore if you make yourself happy, then you make those around you happy, which is the same thing as saying that if you uplift yourself, then you also uplift those around you. Why should this be so? The simple reason is firstly that life is a selfish process, (as opposed to self-centred); and secondly, that there is only one life of which we are all units.

Needless to say, this is a concept which is in direct contradiction to social conditioning, for we have all been taught that you should not be selfish. In other words, "I am not at all selfish, because I always put you first! I always try to make you happy, but you are so selfish that you never make me happy! Sob! Sob! Blame! Blame!"

I don't know about you, but I like being happy! And since I don't like sitting around waiting for free handouts, I prefer to get on with my life and thereby make myself happy. Damn right that is being selfish! But I simply don't care, because through my own experience of being selfish I know how much people love to be with me. Why? Simply because I am happy and, in being happy, they too feel happy just by being around me! And of course, because they are happy, it makes me even more happy, and because I become more happy, they too become more happy! Does that sound conceited? Perhaps it does, but then that will only be because you like to be miserable, because you think that to be miserable is to be humble! But for me, being humble means that I am not so arrogant as to demand that others should make me happy.

The third point we need to look at is that if you give as much as you take, then life expands, the world around us expands and therefore your relationships, instead of being confining and restrictive, become a joyous journey of infinite possibilities. But once again, people are so conditioned into giving, that they give you presents, they give you their expectations, they give you their demands, they give you their problems, they give you their frustration, they give you their anger, they give you their misery and, in short, they give you a huge headache! In fact, people mostly only give in order to tie you up into little knots, for at the end of the day, most so-called giving is only yet another form of manipulation. "I give you so much, but you never give me anything in return!"

People are forever fighting because someone wants to give them something they just do not want. Yet life is not about giving or, for that matter, about taking. Life is instead a process of giving-and-taking. But in practice, people always want only to take, or only to give, and in such a way that it becomes almost impossible to distinguish with any real clarity what is the difference between the two.

So, you want to give me your crossness and bad temper, but you want to take from me joy and happiness; you want to give me your lies and hypocrisy, but you want to take from me honesty; you want to give me your love, to which is attached a whole long string of expectations and conditions, but you want to take from me unconditional love, and I am being unreasonable if I expect you to remember my birthday when you are so busy! Don't you think that is being just a little bit unfair?

You have no right to impose your misery upon the world and then expect everyone else to give you happiness in return. All of us can take anything we want from out of life, provided that there is always a fair exchange of energy. Therefore, because I give much happiness, I can also afford to take happiness wherever I go. And because I choose to learn from everything in my life, I get, as well as take, clarity from everything, and so I can also give clarity wherever I go. It really is as simple as that. I take so that I can give, and I give so that I can take again, and so there is always an exchange of energy, and because of that I never want for anything and, as a result, I am always happy!

Nonetheless, in giving and taking, we should also take care that it really is a fair exchange of energy. In other words, don't try to take more than you give. If you wish to give only a little, then that is alright, as long as you take in return only as much as you have given. If, for example, you are feeling sad, and have only a little joy to give on that day, then give what you have to give, but don't expect everyone around you to shower you with joy in return. We all have our sad moments in life, but even sadness can be beautiful, and therefore life-enriching. Consequently, if you are sad, then you can also share your sadness, you can give your sadness, but remember that you will get sadness reflected back to you. Likewise, if you are angry for some reason, then by all means be angry, give your anger, but then also expect people to respond to you according to what you are giving and, above all, be responsible enough to take as good as you give!

The fourth concept we need to address is that none of us can avoid our fate. This means that if we try to avoid our challenges in life by trying to cut ourselves off from them, we simply become ensnared by those challenges in such a way that we end up feeling like victims. In this respect remember that all of life is merely a system of relationships, of which the most important is the relationship between you and life in general. Therefore if you try to take from life more than you are giving, expect to be miserable.

The reason for this is that all our challenges in life are there so as to enable us to become stronger, wiser, more successful and, in short, happier. So if you are trying to achieve happiness by not facing your challenges, then you are in effect trying to steal happiness!

But we all know what happens to a thief. Sooner or later, zap! You are caught! Consider. You are married, but in always only trying to be happy, you never want to face the challenges that your marriage is presenting to you. In other words, you want to take happiness from your marriage, but you do not want to do anything towards creating that happiness. Then one day, zap! Your marriage is on the rocks, the wheels have come off, and you are facing divorce.

Of course you could always shout out, "Why me, Lord? I only ever wanted to be happy, only ever tried to be happy! It was my spouse who was forever unhappy in our marriage and picking a fight!" Nevertheless, although in all such cases it is always the taker who feels victimised and trapped, the truth of the matter is that it is the taker who is the thief, and thieves should not be allowed to run around stealing from everyone! Therefore if you are being victimised in one way or another, check your taking! For example, if your house is burgled, where in your life are you stealing from others, and in what way? Are you stealing stationery from work? Do you underpay your weekly maid? Do you steal time from your family by not wanting to be at home too often because you don't see eye to eye with your spouse?

Finally, we can now begin to see what is really meant by the third of Captain Life's conditions: we cannot play the blame game, for the whole world is merely our mirror! As a result it does not in any way help to become indignant, to start becoming defensive or to try to justify our actions. By doing so we only reinforce the very things that cause us to be unhappy, since we always get exactly what we strive for! The universe always says, "Yes!" If you want justifications, everyone will give you justifications. If you want to be defensive, everyone will be defensive towards you. If you want to be aggressive, everyone will reflect aggression for you. If you want to steal, everyone around you will steal left, right and center. And if you want to be happy, and are prepared to work for that happiness, you will surround yourself with others who also want to work towards being happy.

THE ART OF LISTENING

To relate implies understanding.

Earlier we touched upon the fact that most people drift through life chasing some rainbow in the sky, and that there are very few indeed who know exactly what will make them happy. However, if we drift it means that we are at the mercy of someone or something else, and if we are chasing a pie in the sky, then, well……

The biggest cause of such behaviour is that none of us have ever been taught how to communicate properly. Consequently, we go through life never being able to express either to others, or especially to ourselves, what it is that is bothering us, or what it is that we would like out of life. However, not being able to communicate effectively means that one cannot relate properly to the world, or to others. But most important of all, it means that you will also not be able to relate to yourself, for if you cannot express even to yourself what will make you happy, then how can you ever hope to be happy? Moreover, if you are not happy, contented and at peace, you will definitely not like yourself very much, and through not liking yourself, you will not want to spend time with yourself. Instead you will always be out and about, desperately trying to escape your own sense of unhappiness, which, in the final analysis, means that you are trying to escape from yourself!

Yet, if you ask a person who is trying to escape from themselves what is wrong, that person will invariably shrug his or her shoulders and say, "Nothing!" This is what we term "undelivered communication", or quite simply the "nothing game". However, the irony in playing the nothing game is that there really is nothing wrong! The only thing that is wrong is that the person concerned does not know what it is to communicate either with him or herself, or with the world out there. Caught up in an endless sense of frustration that cannot be verbalised, but that can only be expressed by constantly being on the run in some way, such a person never finds the happiness they are seeking.

The only way of breaking that debilitating pattern is to learn the art of listening. Very few people ever really listen at all. Why? Because most of the time their low self-images tend to get in the way. As a result, people are either so busy arguing with you and pushing their own point of view that they cannot listen, or alternatively, they are so busy in their heads formulating what they are going to reply to you, that they also cannot listen. Does this sound familiar? If it does, it means you are doing it too!

If one feels bad about oneself because of a low self-image, then anything and everything said to one will be perceived as criticism. For example, if your spouse says to you that she is not happy in your marriage, the chances are that you will immediately start feeling bad about yourself. "Oh

God! I have failed! I'm a bad husband. I'm a poor lover. I'm a bad provider, etc., etc." Feeling somehow inferior and inadequate because you are not making your spouse happy, you will start defending yourself by wanting to justify your actions. Rather than initiating the act of intelligent co-operation by guiding your wife towards communicating as fully as possible what it is she is feeling, or sensing, you instead feel attacked, criticised and you become incapable of listening properly. Conflict has surfaced in a big way, but it is not being used to uncover new knowledge, and it merely turns into more conflict, because your wife is trying to say one thing, and you are "hearing" something else. "I am not saying it is your fault, damn you!" "But you are saying that you are not happy, and since I am the one you are married to, that obviously implies that I cannot make you happy!"

So many relationships end up in a soggy mess because, as a result of feeling criticised and attacked, people always end up pushing points of view which even they are not certain of. In an attempt to defend themselves, (against what, one wonders?), they will generally start making wild statements in an effort to put forward concepts they do not even vaguely grasp, let alone being tried and tested knowledge. Therefore far from conflict leading to intelligent co-operation, and through that to new knowledge, it simply leads to so much garbage and eventually to the divorce court. This same thing of course happens also in other relationships, like for example, the workplace, where your defensiveness and garbage will get you fired!

Learning to listen properly is not at all difficult to do, for it is quite as simple as saying to yourself that you do want to listen to what the other person is saying to you. If you do that, you will find that even if that person is criticising you, you will not fall into the trap of feeling bad about yourself, but will instead become fascinated to see how you really tick in relating to others. By being able to see how you tick, and what makes you tick (or not), you discover that it is really very easy to shift the focus from feeling victimised to feeling empowered.

For example, if someone is accusing you of being cold and aloof, and you really listen in the sense of trying to figure out why he or she should find you aloof, you will without a doubt quickly enough begin to see why. Say your friend tells you that you are aloof because you behave in a distant manner by avoiding physical contact. If you are being honest rather than trying to defend or justify your actions, you will see that your friend is in fact right. Therefore to try and pretend that your friend is wrong will just be plain stupid. So, if you start to look at why you avoid physical contact, the chances are that you will come to realise that it is because, for some reason or other, you feel unlovable. Clearly, far from criticising you, your friend has given you a valuable pointer towards starting to improve your self-image, and thereby also to improve your relationship with others. In short, your friend is helping you to understand yourself better.

Realise that if the people around us do not point out to us what our shortcomings are, we would probably never find out or, at least, never bother to find out. What's more, through the art of listening we not only learn a great deal about ourselves, but if we bear in mind that we too are mirrors for those around us, we also learn a great deal about others by listening to what they tell us about ourselves, about themselves or about someone else.

In trying to develop understanding we naturally come up against what is best termed "unfulfilled expectations". So often, as a result of not really understanding either ourselves, or others, we have wild expectations that have nothing at all to do with the realities posed by life. For example, if you do not like yourself and therefore cannot live with yourself, it is completely unrealistic to expect someone else to like you or to live with you. Likewise, if deep down inside you believe yourself to be inadequate in your job, then it is once again unrealistic to expect your boss to believe in you. Yet this exactly what people do, and then they become upset and feel hard-done-by when they do not get the acknowledgement which they are reluctant to give themselves. There is nothing wrong with expectations, provided you practise the give-and-take principle of life. In other words, if you are hard-working and trustworthy in your job, then it is only fair to expect acknowledgement for your work, and to be justly and fairly compensated for your labour. Likewise, if you enjoy your own company and honestly like yourself, then there will be no need for you to try and impress others by being arrogant, conceited and self-centred, but instead you can reasonably expect others also to like you. Therefore, once again we see how very important it is to get to understand ourselves properly.

It is only possible to harbour unrealistic expectations if we do not practise the mirror concept. Once we acknowledge the fact that others are merely our mirrors, then expectations tend to disappear like mist in the sun. For example, if I befriend a new person on the assumption that he will meet up with my expectations of what a true friend should be, he will without a doubt quickly enough begin to disappoint me in some way or another. If, on the other hand, I befriend that man because I have already seen that he is very much my mirror, I will never fail to enjoy his company, for every time we meet he will show me something about myself. Some of the things he shows me will be positive aspects of myself, which, of course, is why I like him. Others, though, will be negative aspects of myself, which, once again, is why I like to be with him. Through being shown these aspects of myself, I can learn to understand myself, and I can begin to work with both my strong points as well as my shortcomings in a much more conscious way than I would otherwise have been able to do. And what's more, since my shortcomings are my undeveloped potential, I am not going to be disappointed in my friend for showing me my own weaknesses! Nonetheless, if he really is a true friend, he will be just as keen to work on himself as I am, and therefore rather than supporting each other in our bullshit, we are going to be completely open and ruthless with each other!

One final word on mirrors. Sometimes we are shown an old mirror so that we can gain a greater belief in ourselves, and because of this it is important to learn to distinguish with total honesty between what is a present mirror and what is an old mirror. In this respect, remember that our mirrors can never lie to us, and therefore if you change, then so too must your mirror change. However, if you change but your mirror does not change, then that mirror will leave your life or, alternatively, it is necessary for you to leave that mirror in order to gain a greater belief in yourself.

Therefore, if you have in all honesty worked with a mirror every way you can, and you are convinced by your own actions that you have indeed changed, but still your mirror persists in not changing, then rest assured that you are up against an old mirror. In such a case, acknowledge to yourself that that person no longer mirrors for you what you have become. Look at their behaviour and realise that you used to do that, and that you still have the potential to do that, but also acknowledge to yourself that you are no longer guilty of that type of behaviour. If your mirror still persists, it means that you have to claim your power by moving on. If you don't make the move, you will invariably be forced back into your old behaviour patterns, for the simple reason that our mirrors cannot lie!

THE SECRET OF UNCONDITIONAL LOVE

Ruthlessness and unconditional love are synonymous.

The biggest cause of people having a low self-image is the fact that the majority of humanity practices conditional love as opposed to unconditional love. This is a concept we can make as complicated or as simple as we wish. Speaking for myself, I prefer simplicity. So to put it in a nutshell, I term it playing "the nice guy". People are so concerned about being liked or, to be more specific, people are so self-centred and conceited, that they would rather lie than tell the truth. For example, which of your friends will speak to you with total honesty? Alternatively, which of your friends can you address with total honesty? Mostly it is always a question of, "I don't want to tell people my truth because I will hurt them. And if I hurt them they won't love me."

Parents especially perpetuate this dishonesty by teaching their children concepts such as, "If you listen to me and be a good girl, I will buy you a doll for Christmas." So the child keeps pretending to be a good girl or a good boy, even if it is really very wicked when the parent is not watching. In short, the child is being taught to lie about its behaviour, and result of this social lying is, "Just keep telling me what I want to hear, just keep lying to me, and I will buy you a doll, I will be a faithful husband, I will be the best friend you have ever known, I will be the best employee you have ever had."

This dishonesty is what we term conditional love. In other words, "Just lie like me, like I have been taught to lie, and we will all live happily ever after!" However, if such a life is not for you, then realise that the only way to change this is to start practising unconditional love. Unconditional love does not mean that you must love someone even though he is stabbing you in the foot, raping your wife and robbing you of everything you possess. Unconditional love means that you love others enough to give them your truth even if it does mean they are never ever going to speak to you again, or that they end up calling you a mean, horrible bastard. Having such honesty is being ruthless. To be ruthless does not mean being cruel, but it means that you take pity neither on yourself nor on the person you are speaking to.

Once again this concept is in direct contradiction to social conditioning. However, unless you want to be a liar and live a life of lies, you have no option but to start being ruthless with yourself. "If I don't want to be ruthless with others, then it is only because I don't want to be seen as the bad guy!" "I don't want to be ruthless with others because I am a coward!" "If I refuse to be ruthless, I will end up compromising myself!"

Shortly we will look at the difference between compromising ourself and sacrificing something to gain something else. With a compromise, nobody wins.

Most people find it very difficult to be ruthless, and mainly because they feel too bad to use their anger properly. Anger is simply the desire to fight — to fight for what you believe in. So if someone is stabbing you in the foot, then get angry. Don't suppress your anger, just use it to be ruthless! Generally speaking, we fear to express our anger because, according to social conditioning, it is not nice to be aggressive. But the sad truth is that people who try to suppress their anger always end up being extremely aggressive! If, on the other hand, you use your anger when you need to, you will only ever become aggressive when you need to fight. The rest of the time you will be a well-balanced and even-tempered person who is a pleasure to be with.

It is very natural to become ruthless when anger surfaces, for in the face of anger fear retreats, doubts fall away, feelings of inadequacy and inferiority are temporarily forgotten and as a result there is in that moment always great clarity and a very real inner strength.

However, using anger does not mean that you have to scream and shout like a lunatic, or behave like a bull in a china shop. Using your anger means that you allow it to surface and, by not pushing it away, you allow it to guide you into clarity, then into ruthlessness and finally into the appropriate action. So if, for example, your boss is accusing you of not measuring up to your job description, then allow yourself to become angry, not in the sense of not listening, or trying to defend and justify your actions, but in the sense of, "I'm going to fight for this job, therefore let me listen with care!" If you do that, you will hear your boss loudly and clearly and in having that clarity you will know whether it is your own shortcomings or whether it is your boss that you have to fight.

If you use your anger in this way, it will always guide you to new knowledge rather than conflict, and therefore, far from being fired at work, or finding yourself in the divorce court, you will gain in strength and in self-confidence, and because of that, you will also gain the respect of those around you. I have never known any boss to fire an employee who can listen without being defensive, and who also has the backbone and the strength to fight for his or her job. Likewise I have never encountered a marriage that has failed where both people concerned are completely open and ruthless with each other in the sense of fighting to build a good relationship. To be ruthless and to use one's anger constructively is to strive for intelligent co-operation and understanding, both of which are needed in order to have a successful and meaningful relationship, irrespective of whether it is a romantic relationship, a professional relationship or the relationship with oneself.

COMPROMISE VERSUS SACRIFICE

Actions speak louder than words.

The final concept that concerns us here is one which is more often the cause of problems than anything else, namely, broken promises. First of all, know that if you promise anything to anyone, you are laying yourself open to being accused of lying. How can I promise you that I will always stay with you in marriage, or work for you, if I don't know what tomorrow will bring? I can only make a promise if it pertains to the moment. For example, I can stay with you now for who and what you are, and for who and what I am, but should either of us change, I cannot guarantee that I will still want to stay with you, or that you will want to stay with me, for that matter. Likewise, I can promise to work for you now, but what happens if you find someone better to replace me, or if your business goes bankrupt and you can no longer pay me my salary?

Promises are dangerous things, and although they are not bad in themselves, we should realise that it is a lot safer and considerably wiser to base our relationships upon action rather than promises. Therefore, if I am to stay married to you then that will depend upon the action both of us take in order to ensure that our marriage thrives. Similarly, if I am to continue working for you, then that will depend upon the action we both take to ensure that we have a continued working relationship that is mutually beneficial.

Unfortunately though, people tend to base their beliefs more on the strength of promises than in action, and so they always end up compromising themselves in one way or another. Here again we see the need to be ruthless. "Do not promise me that you will never again have an affair, prove it to me through your actions." "Do not promise me you will try harder. Show me!"

If, on the other hand, you find yourself in a position where you are caught in-between the devil and the deep blue sea, then still there is no need to compromise yourself, although you may well be forced into having to sacrifice something. For example, if your wife snores like a chainsaw and keeps you awake all night, ask yourself the question, "Is this marriage more important to me than lying awake all night?" If the marriage means nothing to you, then divorce the woman and marry someone who will coo sweet nothings into your ear all night! But if the marriage is important to you, then don't compromise yourself by lying awake all night, plug your ears, for goodness sake! In this case you will have sacrificed your hearing during the night, but you will be saving a marriage that is important to you.

Compromise! What a wonderful word that is! By making promises to each other, you and I can take our relationship anywhere we wish! Isn't that wonderful. "You just keep promising me you will never hurt me, and I promise you I will never be ruthless with you!" "I know I'm not very good in my job, but I promise to try harder if you promise not to report me to the director!" "I admit I stole your wife's affection, but I promise I will make her hate me if you promise not to tell my wife!" Don't you think compromise is a grand and honourable way to live?

Similarly, if you are having to work very long hours, and you don't like it, ask yourself, "Is this job important to me?" If it isn't, walk out and find yourself an easier job somewhere. But if the job is important, then go and speak to your boss. Don't just sit around feeling sorry for yourself, get moving and initiate the act of intelligent co-operation! Go tell your boss that you are fully prepared to work the long hours because the job is important to you, but can't you both find some sort of a solution for the fact that you feel hard-done-by? Perhaps a raise in salary will make the hours seem less long. Perhaps an extended vacation will make the long hours more worthwhile. Perhaps a promotion will make you feel less discontented. Perhaps just a kick up the butt from your boss will do the trick! In any event, one way or another, there is never any good reason for compromise, although often we have to sacrifice something in order to get what it is we really need or want.

Remember the old proverb here: You cannot (always) have your cake and eat it!

This then brings us to that final question: "What do you want in a relationship?"

This is a question that only you can answer for yourself. No two people are alike, and so what I want will not necessarily be what will make you happy. Therefore, sit down and make a list of the things you honestly believe will make for a good relationship, irrespective of whether it is a romantic relationship, a professional relationship, the relationship with your kids, your family or with your friends. But in making that list, make sure that whatever you write down is specific and measurable. In other words, you yourself must know what you mean and how it can be accomplished in practical terms.

Once that list is complete, make another for what it is you would like in a relationship with yourself. In making this list, realise that whatever you are writing down is in reality a commitment to yourself. So, if you want the relationship with yourself to be a good one, then clearly you are going to have to do all the work! Once you have seen this, you will also come to the realisation that what you wrote down on your list for relationships with others is also your responsibility. If you want to be happy, you must remember that none of us live on an island and therefore we can only ever be really happy if we relate happily and successfully to the world around us. To do this, forget the blame game! Forget feeling sorry for yourself! Forget your social conditioning! Become ruthless with yourself and get stuck into using what you now know in order to change yourself and thereby to change your mirrors!

SIX

TERM 4:
GIVE YOURSELF TIME

Time is the essence of impeccability.

The fourth condition of Captain Life is that "You must cast your watch into the sea". This means that you must give yourself time, for the simple reason that it takes time to break the habits of a lifetime. Yet, if you are ever going to achieve happiness sooner rather than later, you cannot also afford to waste time, in the sense of indulging in your old habits and behaviour. Let us see what this actually means in practice.

Generally speaking we are all willing to give others time, but when it comes to ourselves, we really give ourselves very little. For example, if you are a single person and you have someone coming over to dinner, you will cook, set the table nicely, complete with flowers and candles. But how often, if ever, will you do this for yourself? However, if you do not love yourself, then why should anyone else love you?

If you are ever going to have a meaningful relationship, you must start with yourself. Only by learning to show yourself respect will you have real respect for someone else. So, stop trying to impress others with your dinner and pretty table — instead show them that you live like that all the time, in which case they will respect you for it and will want to be around you. Exactly the same is true of giving yourself time in which to change. If you do this, you will also not expect your mirrors to change every time you snap your fingers! Life is a process and although we make decisions in the moment that are truly life-changing, implementing those decisions in day-to-day life takes time, just as it takes time for a tree to grow after it has been planted. Relationships are in every respect exactly the same as planting trees. They take time to grow and, above all, they need respect, care and nurturing.

SEVEN

THE RULES FOR PLAYING THE GAME OF RELATIONSHIPS

All of life is a system of games. Some games just require more carefully-defined rules than others.

People often look at me with big tearful eyes and ask what they should do to make their relationships work. I always give the same answer, which is simplicity itself: "If you want to enjoy any game and not get disqualified halfway through, then stick to the rules of the game!" Relationships are no different to any other game and the rules for playing this game are very clearly defined. Yet, people are always so amazed, so indignant and so hurt when they get disqualified from the game for having ignored the rules! How's that for logic? But what is even worse is the fact that most people are such terrible spoil-sports. Always insisting on wanting only to win, they take all the fun out of life because they want you to lose just so that they can win.

What then of the rules? I am purposely not going to explain these at length. Why? Because I'm not a spoil-sport! Half the fun of playing the game of relationships is to find out through your own experience what these rules actually mean to you as an individual. None of us are the same – except possibly in stupidity! We are all unique, we all have our own specific value and therefore our own particular style of playing the game of life. That style is your personal signature — the mark you make upon the world and the mark by which you will be remembered. Some signatures are truly beautiful works of art. Some are strikingly neat and clear. Some look like a spider walked through an ink blotch. Some look like .... I don't know what! Some are just plain ugly. But far too many are so very childish — the mark of gross immaturity. You must decide for yourself what your mark upon the world will be — what you would like it to be.

Here then, are the rules for playing the game of relationships, which is but the game of life itself. If you study these rules you will find that I have already given you everything you need to know about how to use these rules. If you use them, they will generate experience, and that experience will be your experience, your knowledge and therefore also your power. So study them, use them and above all, don't forget to have fun! People are so serious about wanting to win that they forget to have fun. It is therefore hardly surprising that they end up being old before their time, become senile and consequently resort to childish behaviour!

Rule One

TAKE RESPONSIBILITY FOR HAVING THIS PERSON IN YOUR LIFE.

It takes two to tango, so stop trying to play the blame game. See your own role in, and your own contribution to, what is happening in your relationship (romantic, professional, etc.)

Rule Two

DON'T TREAT THE OTHER PERSON IN YOUR LIFE ANY DIFFERENTLY THAN YOU WOULD A STRANGER.

Familiarity has a dreadful habit of breeding contempt! Therefore treat your spouse as you would a stranger; also your boss, your kids, your family and your friends. Always treat others politely and with respect, even if you have known them ever since pa fell off the bus.

Rule Three

ACCEPT YOURSELF FOR WHO AND WHAT YOU ARE.

Acknowledge your shortcomings to yourself and remember that they are your passage to power and your ticket to freedom.

Therefore stop trying to pretend you are not your potential. Instead of continuously justifying your behaviour, learn to listen. Most important of all, learn to listen to your heart, your feelings.

Rule Four

ALWAYS LOOK FOR THE POSITIVE. FOCUS ON THE POSITIVE.

Start giving yourself and those around you credit for what you and they are doing right. It is so easy to criticise, to break down, to point out failure. But how often do you praise either yourself or others for a job well done? We all need a pat on the head from time to time to keep believing in ourselves — even you!

Rule Five

ACKNOWLEDGE GENDER ACCORDING TO ITS PROPER POTENTIAL.

If you are a man, then treat the women in your life as females and not as your mother. If you are a woman, then treat the men in your life as males and not as little boys.

Rule Six

COMPRESS TIME.

Learn not to waste time through indulging in your behaviour. Instead, learn to communicate effectively by being open, honest and ruthless. Don't assume that others can smell what you are silently stewing or fuming about.

Rule Seven

BELIEVE IN YOURSELF AND IN OTHERS.

Stop believing that everyone is out to get you. Practise the mirror concept and therefore acknowledge that others are there to help us and not to victimise us!

Rule Eight

MAKE ALLOWANCES FOR THE DIFFERENCES
BETWEEN MALES AND FEMALES.

Rule Nine

LAUGH! LIFE IS FUN!

Learn to see your own actions, physical, emotional or mental, as well as those of others, for what they really are, namely, folly. If you do, you will find yourself laughing a great deal more than crying. People are really very funny creatures, and that includes you!

Rule Ten

KEEP A JOURNAL.

Life is the most important journey you will ever undertake, and every important journey should be carefully logged in a journal. If you do that, you will be surprised at how much you learn about yourself, about others and about life in general. Record everything, even your feelings, emotions, thoughts, dreams and, of course, the date. Dates tend to reveal patterns, like for example, feeling morose around Christmas time, or feeling happy in spring, etc. But the most important thing about keeping a journal is that, by writing everything down, you actually commit yourself to your decisions and therefore you start taking responsibility for your own life.

EIGHT

THE PASSWORD FOR LIFE AND FOR HAPPINESS

Our relationships are always a reflection, a mirror, of our relationship with ourselves. Remember that always. Therefore if we want to be happy, we must first establish a good relationship with ourselves, and through that, become a whole person who is self-sufficient, self-reliant, self-contained and consequently also self-contented. How can anyone ever hope to have a successful marriage if either that person, or his or her partner, or both, are incomplete in themselves? It is simply not possible to have a good relationship with only half a person!

However, notwithstanding this, remember too that we cannot see ourselves for what we really are without a mirror, or several mirrors. Of all the mirrors we need, the most important of all is the mirror which most closely reflects for us our own inner counterpart. This does not necessarily mean that everyone must get married, but it does mean that all of us do need to have a close relationship with someone of the opposite sex, irrespective of whether this is your spouse, a family member, friend, or your boss at work.

To have a close relationship does not mean that you must have a sexual relationship with that person. It simply means that it must be a relationship based upon the principles of intelligent co-operation. In this respect it is wise to bear in mind that most relationships nowadays are based not upon intelligent co-operation, but upon animal lust. Animal lust is great! But we cannot learn too much about ourselves behaving like bucking broncos all day long. To buck away is hugely enjoyable for as long as it takes, but regardless of how much you want to impress others with your bragging, you are still going to have to cope with your lack of happiness afterwards.

Commit yourself to being happy and you will find that in no time at all life will be taking on a very different meaning, a far more enjoyable meaning than it had before. The reason for this is that, like with any commitment, if you are committed, you will also want to show it to the rest of the world. It is quite as simple as that. When you commit to marriage, you are proud to show the whole world your wedding ring, and so it should be with your commitment to happiness, to life and to yourself. None of us have a guarantee on life, or on what life holds in store for us, but one thing we can be certain of is our commitment to ourselves to be happy, "for better or for worse". And so too should it be with our lives and with our relationships within that life.

"For better or for worse", we all have the ability and the right to choose where we are going to place the focus. We place that focus either on, "Life is a bitch, and so is everyone in it"; or we place the focus on, "All the experiences in my life are so many richnesses which I harvest with love and with joy, because each and every one of them yields happiness through the medium of knowledge."

Only once you have embraced your sadness fully and have cried all of your tears can you know the full meaning of real happiness. If we did not have night, how could you ever know the difference between day and night? Likewise, if you have never experienced both success and failure, how could you ever know what it is to be successful, to be happy?

I think you are a truly great person! I don't care if you think you are the very worst person under the sun, and no matter what you have allowed yourself to become. All of that baggage you have buried yourself under is simply behaviour, and behaviour can be changed at any time you choose to do so. I think you are great because you are my mirror! Even if your behaviour stinks, I know I am no better and no worse than you are. Perhaps you are for me an old mirror, but unless I have been there, unless I have been where you are at now, how could I love you? I love you simply because you are me, and I am you, and together we are all units of the one life. Behaviour is one thing and we do not need to accept or to love someone's behaviour. But potential is something else, something precious, valuable, and in each and every case, unique and irreplaceable. I love you for that!

All of life is merely a system of relationships and if you look very carefully you will see that every relationship, regardless of what type it is, is an investment — an investment in yourself! I personally will not invest in anything unless I believe that it is going to be a good investment, that is, one with good dividends. But once I have invested in something, I am also fully committed to my investment, come hell or high water. As a result, when I look at my life, I know that I must have believed this life to be worthwhile as an investment, otherwise I must assume I was pretty dumb! If it is a good investment, then "for better or for worse", I choose to remain fully committed to my investment, to my life and to you. For me personally, it is more pleasurable that way, besides which, I love it, for it is such good fun! For me happiness means having fun, and I have always had fun, even in the saddest moments of my life, and even when the wheels have come off so badly that I was doubtful I would ever find them again. But sad moments come to pass, and the wheels can always again be found. And so the journey goes on — the Journey of Adjustment!

For me the only thing that really matters is that I am real, and that you are real, because then life too is real. This, after all, is the only password we need in order to access life, in order to access happiness. So, if there is a final rule for handling life, for handling relationships, and which sums up all of the others in a nutshell, it is the rule:

BE REAL. MAKE YOURSELF AND OTHERS REAL.

As Captain Life warns us all, not to have that required password, or to try and avoid finding it through life's experience, is to forfeit our lives in one way or another. Some people die physically. Some die emotionally. Some die mentally. Some just die somewhere inside, in that the spark has gone from their lives, from their eyes and from their hearts. These are the walking dead who are never real, but who are like so many phantoms passing through our lives. I see these phantoms, and yet it is not possible to have a relationship with a passing shadow. In order to have a relationship, it must be with a being who has substance, flesh, bones and, above all, a heart! In other words, to have a relationship with someone means that that person must be real. Nothing else matters, for it can all be changed during the Journey of Adjustment.

ALSO BY THÉUN MARES AND AVAILABLE SOON

UNVEIL THE MYSTERIES OF THE FEMALE
―――――― & ――――――
ACCESSING THE POWER OF THE VOID – A QUEST OF MALENESS

As a result of trying to correct the mistakes of the past, men have now become weak and disempowered, and women, having had to fight for acknowledgement within society, have lost touch with their femininity through the pursuit of male-like qualities. This problem is becoming worse as society encourages people to be more and more uni-sexual. Men and women are indeed equal, but nonetheless they represent opposite polarities that are unique in their qualities, each having different functions and purposes. Humanity has lost this knowledge, and consequently the true roles of the male and female have become distorted.

It is not surprising then that people today are so very confused about what it means to be a man and what it means to be a woman, or that the concepts and the implications of the terms male and female, masculine and feminine are also misunderstood.

Nowadays we are constantly being shown that women can do most of the things that men once considered their prerogative, and vice-versa. However, simply to change roles is not the solution. Unless we understand what it means to be male and what it means to be female, we will still be left with each sex feeling isolated and marginalised, as each struggles to find its identity through the opposite sex.

In these books Théun Mares dispels the myths born of social conditioning, and attempts to put men and women back in touch with true masculinity and femininity.

THE TOLTEC TEACHINGS SERIES BY THÉUN MARES

This series of books provides more of a technical background to the concepts introduced in this book. Toltec means 'a man or women of knowledge', and since true knowledge only comes out of life experience the Toltec tradition developed as a practical approach to life, focusing on practical issues that arise in our everyday lives.

RETURN OF THE WARRIORS
CRY OF THE EAGLE
THE MISTS OF DRAGON LORE

REVIEW COMMENTS:

- Conscious Living – Australia — "Without a shadow of a doubt, this book's clarity offers a wide path to intellectual freedom, spiritual joy and utter personal power"
- Napra ReView – USA — "This is deep, intense, rewarding material, ultimately leading to the achievement of true freedom and empowerment.
- Magical Blend Magazine – USA — "Amazingly clear and jargon-free... a unique introduction to the subject-matter."

READER COMMENTS:

- "The work is clear, well-written and highly-informative"
- "...I have begun to apply practical techniques to every moment of my life. Already, only after several months, I have noticed subtle, and yet for me, dramatic effects."
- "The path of this philosophy is useful in my daily life and is not escapist in any way".
- "...amazed at the difference the practices have made in my life".

INSTITUTE FOR THE STUDY OF MAN

Practical courses and workshops.

Elizabeth Schnugh is director and founder of the Institute for the Study of Man, which provides practical courses based on the concepts contained in this book.

Her ten-year experience as financial director of a large multinational company convinced Elizabeth that a radical change was needed in the ways we do things, as well as in the ways in which we relate to each other, and life.

She has been working closely with Théun over the past few years to design and present a series of courses with the emphasis on providing people with tools with which to uplift themselves and to change their lives.

Elizabeth says: *The bottom line for every single person is to believe that they do have the answers for themselves. We teach people to address the issues in their lives from where they originate, rather that treat the symptoms. What this boils down to is handling relationships, for at the end of the day all of life is about relationships. We give people practical tools to transform all types of relationships, and we address them at all levels.*

For further details, as well as information on organising courses in your country, please contact:

INSTITUTE FOR THE STUDY OF MAN
PO Box 2294
Clareinch
7740
Cape Town – South Africa

Telephone: +27 21 683 5892
Fax: +27 21 683 0084
E-mail: elizs@iafrica.com
Website: www.uplift.co.za

ORDERING OUR BOOKS:

Order our books from your favourite bookstore.

Alternatively, detailed ordering information, as well as online purchase options, can be found on our website:
www.elusivehappiness.com

For direct sales in England and neighbouring areas call:

Telephone: +44 1825 723398
Fax: +44 1825 724188

Otherwise please contact us directly.

Lionheart Publishing
Private Bag X5
Constantia 7848
Cape Town
South Africa

Telephone: +27 21 794 4923
Fax: +27 21 794 1487
E-mail: cajmi@iafrica.com
Web: www.elusivehappiness.com

Come and visit our website for interesting articles, new insights into handling relationships, as well as online advice and sharing of experiences in our discussion forum.